CONTENTS

Acknowledgements

So many people have contributed to this book. I am sincerely grateful to every one of them for their memories, their old photographs, for every single item which has built up the story of the history of our parishes.

It would take too long to list the names of all the people who have lent pictures and who have given up their time to describe the villages as they were and the changes they have seen.

Over 200 people have been involved. I am grateful for their patience, as I have returned with more questions, wanting dates of events and asking about faces in photographs. I am constantly astonished by the ability of folk to identify people in pictures, some taken between 60 and 80 years ago.

I am indebted to you all, to present-day residents who grew up here and to those people who have moved away, corresponded with me and even travelled back to bring their contributions of images and recollections.

The compilation of this book would not have been possible without the huge amount of work done by my husband, David, in copying and collating many hundreds of pictures, and I am immensely grateful for his help and support.

Pictures which could not be used in the book because of limits on space will feature in future 'Old Blofield' exhibitions at village events, so that the 1,200 images we have been shown may all be appreciated.

To all who have turned out the cupboards of your homes and the cupboards of your minds, I wish to thank you for making this a resource for the future, an account of evolving village life, aspects of which we may never see again.

Harvesting in Blofield in the 1920s.

4

Introduction

A display in Blofield Church of pictures and their accompanying captions regarding the history of the church and its links with the village was the beginning of a growing exhibition entitled 'Old Blofield'.

As people visited the exhibition, commented, added more information and brought me more old pictures, both the displays and the interest grew. Football teams from way back, groups of school-children, street scenes as they once were, old farming methods and machines, all aspects of life in the parishes were being revealed.

Soon I was taking a tape recorder on visits to older residents to collect their memories.

At events in the church the chancel would be filled with photographs, descriptions and many people taking an interest. Then came the comment: 'You should make it into a book'. Here is the result. Thank you to everyone who has made it possible.

Barbara Pilch, 2006

Map of Blofield and Hemblington parishes.

Three scrapers and an arrowhead.

Left to right, top row: *Lady's pipe, Samian ware, Westerwald stoneware with blue stripes (1580), Roman grey handle, handle (1500);* middle row: *medieval wig curler, Saxon plate edge;* front row: *glass clothes smoother (date unknown), piece of Grimston ware tile (700 years old), tiger ware (1460–1550), handle (date unknown).*

❖ CHAPTER 1 ❖

Early History

The parishes of Blofield and Hemblington lie between Norwich and the Norfolk Broads, with miles of sandy coastline a short distance away.

In former times Mousehold Heath stretched all the way from St James in Norwich to the northern part of the village, which is called Blofield Heath.

Clearly Blofield was once a much more watery place. In 1294 Sir Robert de Catheston asked for the right to fish and cut reeds in any part of the 'great pool of Blofield' and in 1542 there were salt marshes and fisheries here.

The higher water table in the fourteenth century meant that the valley between Braydeston and the church in Blofield was sufficiently flooded to allow Caen stone to be floated on barges close to the building site for a new church which was to replace an older church on the same site, probably using some of the materials from the previous building.

The medieval church we know, was built large, as a church befitting the Bishop of Norwich, whose country palace was in Blofield.

This easterly corner of England was the most densely settled area, wealthy from the wool industry, and the size of the church, the largest in the Blofield Hundred, reflects that fact. It could be said that the church is indeed 'built on bales of wool'.

In 1732 Edmund Harley, second Earl of Oxford, travelling in the eastern counties, described the Blofield countryside as 'worthy to have been imitated by the famous landscip painter Gasper Poussin.'

In the gently undulating countryside, valleys with streams were settled as far back as Mesolithic times – 3,000–4,000BC. Archaeological finds in a valley at Hemblington point to habitation with potteries and trading posts. Such artefacts as arrowheads, discovered at plough depth, an axe head dating from the middle stone age and three pot-boiling sites show where people lived and cooked.

They would have a fire constantly alight and would heat pots of water by placing into them heated flint stones, called pot boilers, the pots themselves being too fragile to be placed on a fire.

Remnants of pottery made elsewhere in Britain, and in Germany and Italy, suggest much movement of peoples many centuries ago.

The finding of Samian ware indicates that a Roman villa once stood here – a few Roman building tiles are found amongst the flints in the walls of Hemblington Church. It is thought that a community to the east of the church was struck by plague, the survivors moving away to Pedham.

Old field names tell us of a time gone by; the 'Cator' where carts assembled, the 'Kitchen Piece',

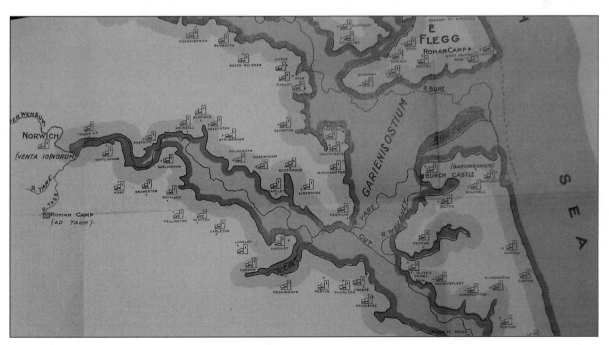

A map of Norfolk during Roman occupation shows the wider river courses and large estuary. It indicates where the medieval churches were later built, on the higher ground. Note that Yarmouth did not exist.

the 'Shoe Swine Piece' and 'Walnut Tree Pightle'.

On Hemblington Hill the 'Pightle' is the site of a fifteenth-century pottery which used clay from nearby marl pits. Boulder clay found here was used for brick making near the blacksmith's shop.

Part of Walsham Wood, which forms the shape of a cross, is named the 'Hangings', where there are two 1,000-year-old oak trees. It is said that carts brought prisoners from Norwich gaol out here to be hanged. Areas in the 80-acre wood had been dug out for peat and in the middle was a huge bog, where the bodies were thrown.

Blofield must once have been an important place, giving its name to both the deanery and to the Blofield Hundred, a subdivision of the county with its own court. This extended nearly 13 miles out from St Michael at Plea Church in the parish of Tombland (formerly called Ratone) in Norwich. Its parishes were Blofield, Braydeston, Brundall, Buckenham, Burlingham St Andrew, St Edmund and St Peter, Cantley, Freethorpe, Hassingham, Limpenhoe, Lingwood, Great and Little Plumstead, Postwick, Southwood, Strumpshaw, Thorpe St Andrew and Witton.

The Domesday Book
The life of these communities has been recorded since the Domesday Book, when the name Hemblington was spelled 'Hemelingetum' or 'Hemelintuna', and 'Blafelda' meant a site near a river.

Other settlements with the prefix 'Bla', such as Blakeney, Blakenham and Blaxham, are all seated by some considerable water, as are Blore and Blonorton. As the first part of Blonorton's name comes from the French *bel eau*, beautiful water, perhaps we can assert that we are at a beautiful riverside site.

Other possible derivations of the names 'Blafelda' or 'Blawefelle' are *Blaa* in Icelandic, meaning yellow, or the Anglo Saxon *Bleoh* or *Bleo* for blue – woad grown locally was used to dye wool. The initial syllable may be Anglo Saxon for to blow, bloom or blossom, and so may imply a neighbourhood remarkable for the richness and beauty of its vegetation. The Anglo-Saxon *feld* or Danish *felt* implies a field, pasture or plain, or an open neighbourhood.

So the picture we have is of a pleasant, fertile place with a river nearby.

Foundation

Imagine the scene: an estuary stretched up to Blofield, this arm of the sea reaching the site where the church was to be rebuilt in the 1380s, to which barges brought the Caen stone used, along with the local flint, in its construction.

Workmen, artisans and craftsmen toiled for many years to construct our lofty church building, and in 1427 it was ready to be consecrated by the bishop.

The tower was added in the following years,

Roose of Blofield providing in his will of 1431 for the fabric of the 'new steeple'.

Lords of the manor
The Manor and Patronage of Blofield were held by the bishops from 1047 until they passed to King Henry VIII in 1535. In 1542 he granted them to Sir Thomas Paston, in whose family they remained for many years.

The Paston family
One of the earliest Pastons we know much about was Clement Paston, who lived in the village of Paston, 17 miles north-east of Norwich, and died in 1419. The Pastons became important landowners in Norfolk during the fifteenth century, and life at that time is well described in the Paston letters, a series of communications between members of the family covering wide-ranging subjects. This collection of letters began in the lifetime of Clement's son, William Paston I (1378–1444), when Henry VI was king.

Written by clerks, servants, friends or domestic chaplains, what is unusual about these letters is that so many of them have survived. About 1,000 were written, telling us of anxiety, fear, triumph, love and business matters, of domestic details such as health and food, local feuds and affrays.

Through them we also learn about such diseases as the plague. In 1471, Sir John Paston II wrote to his brother, John Paston III: 'I fear that there is great death in Norwich and in other towns in Norfolk. I assure you that it is the most wide spread death *[plague]* that there ever was in England.' In 1479 John Paston III begs his brother for a remedy:

I ask you to send me, with the next man who comes from London, two pots of treacle from Genoa. They will cost 16 pence for I have used that which I had… I ask you to do it quickly. Many people are dying in Norwich and especially round my house.

The wool trade
The Norfolk wool trade expanded in the 1300s and woollen cloth, woven on horizontal looms in workshops, became an important export. The dyes were made from such plants as woad, madder, weld and lichens.

In the fifteenth century most ordinary people owned few clothes which, hand made, were expensive. When Sir John Paston III ordered two new pairs of hose they cost him as much as would eight sheep. Most clothes were made from wool.

The English woollen textile industry in the Middle Ages was very important, made much money for this part of England and employed many people in the spinning, weaving and dying of woollen cloth.

Paston tombs
Wealthy people such as the Pastons were willing to

Edward Paston, his wife, six sons and three daughters shown at prayer on the large wall memorial.

Dryden's epitaph to Margaret Paston.

pay for an expensive tomb for an important member of the family. In 1478 Sir John Paston II planned to sell 12 yards of gold cloth to the king and use the money to put a tomb over his father's grave: 'There shall be none like it in Norfolk.'

A large wall memorial in Blofield Church shows Edward Paston with his wife and children at prayer.

Edward died in 1630. He had settled on himself for life, with the remainder to his son Thomas, for his life, the manor of Paston, Thorpe-by-Norwich, Blofield and several marshes, besides property in Suffolk and Norfolk.

John Dryden, poet laureate

John Dryden, the first poet laureate, wrote a touching epitaph in stone to the wife of another Edward Paston, Margaret, who died aged 23.

Dryden, poet laureate to both Charles II and James II, was appointed by Charles II and worked closely with the king to 'rhyme the confusion of his enemies', rewarded only with the laureateship and the promise of £100 a year and 'one butt or Pype of the best Canary Wyne.' By the time Margaret's epitaph was published in a book of poetry some of the wording had been altered, so that Dryden scholars are still excited to discover the stone memorial on the floor of Blofield Church's chancel – a first edition of the poet's work.

Dryden's connection with Norfolk came via his wife, Lady Jane Howard, whose niece, Lady Anne, had married Margaret Paston's maternal uncle, Henry Bedingfield, second Baronet of Oxburgh Hall.

The Drydens, Pastons, Bedingfields and Framptons were united by the bond of their Roman Catholicism. Dryden's wife was probably already a Catholic at the time of their marriage in 1663, and the poet converted to Catholicism in around 1685.

David Hopkins, MA PhD, Professor of English Literature at Bristol University, on visiting the epitaph, stated that: 'It has been plausibly suggested that he wrote the "Epitaph on Margaret Paston" at the request of his wife's relatives, possibly on a visit to Norfolk.'

Dryden was the only poet laureate to be sacked!

When the Protestant William III came to the throne in 1689 he required all holders of high office to take an oath of allegiance. This Dryden, now a Catholic, refused to do and his appointment was not renewed.

Turbulent times

During the turbulent times of Charles I and II and the Commonwealth a rector at Blofield, Alexander Shipdham, wrote of the great difficulties of keeping church registers. These had been kept since 1538, when it was ordained that 'in all churches should be kept a register of every Wedding, Christening and Burial within the same parish forever.'

In 1660, however the rector was bemoaning the fact that any reader:

… findest this register in all parts imperfect seeing the abominable destruction of this kingdom caused by unnatural and bloody war between his Majesty Charles the first of ever blessed memory, and his most unhappy parliament which had ruined him and his kingdom and finally murdered him in a most barbarous manner before his own gates at Whitehall.

Woollen shrouds

By the reign of Charles II Blofield's rector, Charles Reve, was explaining the Act of Parliament which

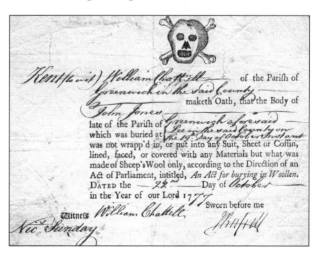

A certificate for 'burying in woollen'.

9

insisted on the 'burying in woollen' shrouds rather than in those of flax, hemp, silk, hair, gold or silver, an Act designed to help the wool trade to flourish.

A bishop's palace in Blofield

The bishops of Norwich once had a country residence in Blofield which was referred to as their palace, or manor house, as they then held the manor.

Thomas Percy, Bishop of Norwich, is known to have died in the residence on 8 August 1369. A park sold to Sir Thomas Paston in 1542 was no doubt part of the bishop's property and the palace became Sir Thomas's residence.

Although all traces of the palace or manor house have disappeared, it seems likely that it stood to the south of the church and that a deer park to provide winter food ran from south of the church as far as the stream which forms the boundary with Braydeston.

It is said that the site of the bishop's palace subsequently became a brick-making field, and eighteenth- and nineteenth-century maps show the area to the south of Church Road and east of Bay Bridge as Brick Kiln Meadow.

The manor of Blofield

The Paston family were lords of the manor until 1713, when it passed to the Burkin family. On Dina Burkin's marriage to Jeremiah Burroughes in 1763 it passed via the Burroughes family to Henry Negus Burroughes, who owned the Burlingham estate in the early-twentieth century. His loss of his land through gambling meant that the large estate was sold in 1919.

The patronage of the rectory passed down with the manor. In 1736 Thomas and Mary Heath of Hemblington conveyed the advowson (right of presentation to a benefice) to the Master and Fellows of Gonville and Caius College, Cambridge. Until 1995 they were the patrons who appointed the incumbent to the benefices of Blofield and Hemblington patronage. In that year the patronage was suspended.

Gonville and Bateman

In 1349 Edmund Gonville, rector of Terrington, in Norfolk, founded a hall in Cambridge bearing his name. On his death in 1351 his executor, Bishop Bateman, finished the foundation. Bateman had also founded Trinity Hall in 1350.

Bishop Bateman has a close connection with Blofield Church and is commemorated on the parapet of the tower and also in the west window. It is possible that he raised money for the building of the church.

Village life

In 1837, just a month into the reign of Queen Victoria, Blofield saw its young men being incited to riot and disturbance. It was election year and some of the Norwich candidates were bent on disrupting their opponents' campaigns. At the Swan Inn at Blofield local constables began recruiting men who were given a shilling and the further promise of 5s. a day and their maintenance if they would go to Norwich in gangs, armed with bludgeons, to create riot and disturbance.

Why the men of our parishes? Well, this was a 'town in which a number of athletic young men are much in the practice of camping, wrestling and such other games.'

Village activities once included handbell ringing, and there were Whitsuntide sports which included a mile run along the turnpike from the milestone near Witton to that at the east end of Blofield.

Blofield hiring sessions were traditionally held a few days before Old Michaelmas.

A post road map, 1820.

CHAPTER 2

Schooldays

As early as 1349 it is recorded that 'the Bishop collated, to the mastership of the grammar school in this town, William Bunting.'

Traditionally, the parish priest, probably the only person in the village to know any Latin, would take on a few scholars, and Blofield Church porch had an upper room which was once used as a schoolroom. A porch was often the safest place in the village for a library, treasury or schoolroom, being much less likely to burn down than a domestic building, and anyone who broke in, thus committing sacrilege, would face awful punishment.

And so, in Blofield's upper room, the Revd Charles Reve, rector from 1671, taught a few scholars of the village. On his death in 1727 he left provision for Beech House, opposite the church, to be used as a school for the education of village children.

The money Revd Reve left in trust continued to help village people and by 1906 was providing:

£9 as rewards to school children, £6.10s. as part mainte-nance of one boy during Apprenticeship, £2.12s. bill for bread, £1.15s. for three widows' gowns, £4 paid to the poor at Christmas and £34.10s. to Gedge for New Well.

The History of Education in the Villages
by David Pilch

The passing of the Education Act of 1870 marked a sea change in the nation's education. Prior to this governments had no rôle in schooling, the quality of which was largely determined by social status and income and ranged from the early foundation of public schools to village dame- or day-schools, whose teachers needed no educational qualifications or ability.

The Act of 1870 inaugurated universal compul-sory elementary education. The upper limit of fees was 9d. a week but this could be waived in cases of hardship. It was not until 1918 that fees were abol-ished and the leaving age set at 14 years.

On the passing of the 1870 Act, boards were set up and schools soon became established in towns and cities. In rural areas, however, the progress was much slower, which became a source of scandal. Thus it was only on the issue of a final notice, on 23 September 1874, by the Department of Education, that the first meeting of the Blofield United District Board finally took place on 24 June 1875.

The first meeting, at the Parish Church, adjourned to the Globe inn, where subsequent meetings were held in a private room.

The first elected board members were William Heath Jary, Esq., elected chairman; Mr Edward Gilbert, elected vice chairman; Mr William Larke Cooke, Robert Deary Rix and Benjamin Sutton. Mr Herbert Cole was appointed clerk at £25 per annum.

One School Instead of Two?
The board was soon in conflict with the Education Department inspector, Revd Francis Synge, who

The school at Beech House before 1878. The boy on the far left is wearing a belted tunic of the late 1850s or '60s.

One plan was to build the board school at Callow Green.

wanted to know why the board was proposing to establish only one school in Blofield 'in lieu of the two notified to them to be requisit by The Education Department.'

The notice of 23 September 1874 had required the establishment of a school for 122 children in the southern part of the village and one for 127 children by Hemblington Corner for those in the northern part. In spite of this, the board continued to petition for a single school in the Callow Green area, arguing that this would be equidistant, no child having more than 1½ miles to walk. It also claimed it would be easier to staff one school with a master than two with less qualified mistresses. However, one cannot help but suspect that the burden on the ratepayers of two schools was also a factor.

Two schools ordered

This tried the patience of the education authorities, who pointed out that by siting the school between the two centres of population all the children would have a distance to walk and might be reluctant to leave 'the dame schools that were popular and inefficient in the parish.' They insisted on two schools but did allow the board, if it insisted, to increase the proportion of children attending the southern school. Boys would thus attend this larger school under a master, the smaller northern school being kept mainly for girls and infants.

Buying land and starting building

Thus, at a meeting on 16 August 1875, the board resolved to build two schools; one for 190 pupils in the south of Blofield (Blofield Board School) on land belonging to Dr Eade near the Town Well; another for 57 children in the north (Hemblington Board School) on a piece of land known as The Ramplings, owned by Mr C.E. Tuck of Norwich. Mr John Pearce was appointed architect. There were delays in buying the southern site, Dr Eade initially being unwilling to sell, but eventually he received £205 for his land and Mr Tuck £37.10s. for his. Other Norfolk schools formed the basis for the plans; Felmingham for Blofield and Spooner Row for Hemblington.

Blofield builder John Withers secured the contract to build the schools at a cost of £3,200, which was funded by a Public Works loan repaid through the rates. Fees were set at 2d. per week for parishioners and 9d. for non-parishioners.

Staff

Advertisements placed for a master and mistress for Blofield and a mistress for Hemblington resulted in the appointment of Mr and Mrs Davies and Miss Walker. However, the Davies, much to the annoyance of the board, withdrew, and so George Mower and his sister Martha were appointed to Blofield. An attendance officer, Mr James Rayner of Brundall, was appointed. His job was 'to visit parents of children not attending and require them to send them.' He would also report on financial or health problems so that fees could be remitted and in some cases birth certificates paid for by the board. Attendance at dame-schools was sometimes used as an excuse for non-attendance.

Work begins

Both schools opened on 1 January 1878 and soon both halls and grounds became popular for other uses. In April the Blofield Corps of Volunteers was given permission to 'drill' on the playground but would be 'held responsible for any damage accidental or otherwise'. Gospel meetings were held at Hemblington School by George Easter and at Blofield by Miss Cameron. Concerts and a tea party were organised by Mr Weston in aid of the restoration of Hemblington Church.

Problems

It soon became apparent that the government's original proposals for the schools were more appropriate than the board's compromise suggestions. Six months after Hemblington School opened the inspector reported that it was oversubscribed – squeezing in 80 children where the capacity was 60 – while 122 attended Blofield, which had a capacity of 190. Moreover, those children who could not be accommodated at Hemblington were choosing to go to the nearer schools at South Walsham or Little Plumstead rather than face the long walk to Blofield. Not only was this costing the board 9d. a week per child in fees to these schools, they were losing the income of 2d. a week per child.

The board decided to remedy the situation by charging children 9d. a week (the maximum permitted) to attend Hemblington School in order to induce them to attend Blofield at only 2d. This produced a public outcry at a meeting held at Hemblington School. Interestingly, the hirer of the school for this meeting – under the guise of an education meeting – was Mr Sutton, a dissenting board member. As a result of the meeting a petition was sent to the Privy Council. This body failed to sanction the board's action but did allow a temporary change to the entry criteria that granted admission to girls and infants only; boys over eight years were not to be admitted. Mr Sutton at first tried in vain to get other board members to agree to enlarge Hemblington School, but in time they agreed and in April 1879 the Department of Education accepted a plan to enlarge the school to take 110 pupils. One feels there must have been an element of 'we told you so' in their approval.

The work was again entrusted to John Withers, and perusal of the board's minute-book reveals that he was kept busy over the years with such problems as 'the unsatisfactory state of the boy's 'offices' (toilets)', problems with the ventilation, draughty windows, cracked arches and the like. Both schools have continued to adapt successfully to changing needs over the years.

Blofield School, 1905.

The early years in both schools

In the early years of both schools classes were large by today's standards. In addition to the master, mistress and assistant teachers, older children were recruited to help with the teaching as monitors. After a time monitors could become pupil teachers, trained by the headmaster of the school. This meant that, besides teaching a class and administering the school's affairs, the head spent some hours each week teaching the pupil teachers how to teach.

In February 1878: 'Herbert Wright (Hemblington School) and Benjamin Merrison (Blofield School) to be appointed monitors in these schools at a weekly salary of one shilling each.'

In October 1882: 'Rebecca Redgement aged 14 years appointed a temporary monitress at a salary at one shilling per week in this school (Blofield) under Act 85 New Code 1882.'

Monitors could also progress to become pupil teachers as apprentices. Benjamin Merrison did this, and the board's minute-book records:

Benjamin Merrison being in attendance, the Articles of Agreement binding his son Benjamin Winter Merrison a Pupil-Teacher in the Blofield Board Schools for a term of four years at a salary of £2.10s. per quarter in the first year, and such sum to be increased by £2.10s. per annum in each subsequent year of the engagement; was next read to him and his son, who both assented to and executed same. Whereupon it was Ordered that the Seal of the Board be affixed to the Articles of Agreement between the Board and Benjamin Merrison and Benjamin Winter Merrison binding the latter Pupil Teacher in the Blofield Board School for four years from the 1st day of July 1878.

Benjamin served his articles and was awarded a testimonial by the board. Not all pupil teachers were recruited locally; applicants to Hemblington School in 1878 were girls of 15 years old from Surrey, Southampton and North Walsham.

School Life

Teaching resources were relatively scarce. At one HMI inspection the comment was: '... the class one children must have used the reading book for a considerable time as they know the contents by heart.' Generally, reports were complimentary about what was being achieved in writing, arithmetic, geography and religious education.

Later, some practical lessons were introduced. With a leaving age of 14, the older pupils were taught carpentry, drawing, gardening, needlework and cookery to prepare them for work. Many went into service or onto the land.

Blofield School became the local centre for woodwork and cookery tuition. Initially, cookery was taught in the Reading Room but later a wooden hut was built and boys and girls walked from Strumpshaw and Lingwood schools for their lessons.

Fires were generally lit in October but in September 1912 the classroom temperature was 51 degrees and the children, it was reported by an HMI, were 'very cold and miserable but the fire had not been lighted.'

Precautions were taken against the cold of winter. Mike Nicholls's grandfather, as a boy, would have goose fat rubbed on in November. His vest and pants would be stitched together, with openings back and front, and would not come off until April.

With the children walking quite long distances to school, bad weather caused problems. At Hemblington, in 1899, a severe snow storm meant that 'only 15 children were present... as soon as it abated the children were sent home for the day, it being inadvisable to allow them to sit in their wet clothes.'

Outbreaks of chickenpox, diphtheria, measles, whooping cough, scarlatina and scarlet fever, mumps and typhoid fever kept children, and sometimes staff, away from school. In 1897 at Blofield:

... a very large number of children who are at present attending school are far from being well the school

ringing from time to time with the continual coughing of the children.

The principle complaint is influenza with here and there a child who has the whooping cough. Under these circumstances the work of the school has been rather handicapped. The teachers however have bravely bore up.

Other reasons for absence varied from 'acorning' in the autumn, fruit gathering in the summer, gleaning after harvest, minding the baby for mother and, for the lads, drilling barley or leading the drill horse.

Children also truanted to watch the hiring sessions or attend the annual fair in the village.

Sometimes parents were difficult

Mrs S. came to school respecting her daughter who had been stayed for misconduct during school hours. Mrs S. was in a terrible temper and entirely refused to hear what had to be said. 'Raging and Storming, she came to school; Raging and Storming, she left.'

Accidents could happen

In 1880:

A series of accidents occurred in the school... In raising the desks according to order, Clara Garrod got her left thumb in the crevice of desk and got it completely smashed. Sent her to the doctor's directly, who dressed and attended to the wound. Shortly after the before mentioned occurrence Jessie Trett fainted and had to be

attended to; while in the afternoon Gerard Postle's nose suddenly set out bleeding – Tuesday being altogether an unlucky day.

For many years Mr William Lightfoot Hague of Garden Road, Blofield, was the attendance officer for both schools, making sure all five-year-olds were registered and keeping an eye on any difficulties at home with which the schools might help.

Time off school

Occasionally school closed for half a day for treats such as parties or outings from Blofield or Hemblington Church Sunday schools, the Methodist chapel or Mission Hall or the Cuttons Corner chapel.

In 1911 Mrs Harker, from Blofield Hall, invited children from both schools to take part in a day of Red Cross displays and the coronation of King George saw more fun at the Hall.

On Wednesday, July 5th, the children attending the schools of Blofield, Hemblington, Little Plumstead and Strumpshaw, numbering about 350, were entertained at the Hall, through the kindness of the High Sheriff and Mrs Harker.

Sometimes the Master at Hemblington took a week off to attend the Norfolk Infantry Volunteer Brigade at Colchester and Mr Mower at Blofield liked to attend military camps of the volunteer corps in the Yarmouth area.

Holidays at harvest time were set by the local

Blofield School, 1914. Far left, back row: William Lightfoot Hague *(attendance officer); second from right, front row:* Cyril Hague. *The boy wearing a cap has ringworm and has had his head shaved.*

Mrs Rope with her class of five to seven-year-olds in 1920/21. First on left, back row: *Jack Gedge;* fifth from left, front row on chairs: *Peggy George.*

farmers, who needed entire families to help in the fields. Even young children could carry 'elevenses' and 'fourses' to the fields for their fathers. In 1915 school broke up on 13 August and returned after harvest on 20 September. If there was a delay in bringing in the crops the school holiday was extended.

The rector visited regularly and gave out prizes each year to the children with the best attendance record, the Reve fund financing these awards.

By the first half of the twentieth century young teachers were travelling to Blofield and Hemblington schools from Norwich, sometimes arriving late because of missed trains and long wet walks from Brundall Station.

As a pupil Ivy Hanton (later Stone) walked a mile and a half from her home in Brundall. At lunchtime she had from 12 noon to walk home, eat and return to school for lessons at 1p.m. Children who came from further afield might stay in school and eat food they brought with them. For them, in the winter, cups of Horlicks could be bought for a halfpenny.

Pupils and teachers at Blofield School

Charlie Howes remembers that: 'The headmaster, Mr Foreman, was very strict. I remember he always wore plus fours.'

Headteachers at Blofield School

Mr George Mower 1878
Mr Foreman 1919
Mr Golder 1934
Mr Mattocks 1946
Mr George 1953
Mr Eric Bacon 1958
Mr Chris Clements 1981

Eric Bates's journey to school from his home in Globe Lane was often exciting. Using his mother's bike, he would gather friends as he went along, ending up with six boys clinging on. He would pedal the bike while David Rope sat on his shoulders, John Ward might be on the carrier, and three boys from Shiels Court boys' home would take up position on the pins at the front facing backwards, between the saddle and handlebars and making a second on the carrier. As they gathered speed down the hill they hoped that the gate into the playground would be left open!

For a while in the 1950s the children, instead of leaving school aged 14, attended Hillside Avenue School until they were 15. Minter's taxi took them, picking up three or four children in Blofield and collecting a few more from Blofield Heath.

Eric refused to go to Hillside and turned up for his final year at Blofield School. What did they do with him? Well, he spent a lot of time looking after the garden and the school bees. He was already keeping

15

The school Red Cross Links group was taught by Miss Newton, 1935. Left to right, back row: *Eileen Platten, Dorothy Saunders, Sylvia George, Jean Merrison, Joyce Patterson, Edna Beck;* middle row: *Daisy Bussey (later Norton), Joyce Norton, Eva Barrett, Helen Grass, Audrey Cork, Lena Laws, Winnie James, Mary Brown;* front row: *Nancy Gibbs, Doreen Payne, Eileen Guppy, Rita Platten, Lorna Ribbans, Joan Grass, Violet Alden.*

The athletics team, c.1949–50. Left to right, back row: *Janet Watson, Vivian Hewson, Michael Able, Michael Slack, Ann Hales, Margaret Alison, David Ferra, Ray Marsh, Michael Cushion, Gillian Rope, Ann Delf;* middle row: *Dennis Wymer, John Debbage, Grahame Baynes, David Dale, Roy Debbage, Peter Gill, Douglas Horner, Derek Buxton;* front: *Barbara Satterley, Judy Marshall, Jennifer Dale, Dorothy Bates, Monica Dye, Mabel Howlett, Muriel Howard.*

The football team, 1950. Left to right, back row: E. Bates (captain), R. Rope (V. Captain), J. Wordingham, E. Flood, M. Theobald; middle row: C. Pratt, M. Jones, A. Parker, D. Reynolds, D. Marsh; front row: P. Pauley, M. Gilder, B. Fuller.

Canteen staff in 1948. Left to right: Mrs Francis, Mrs Woodrow (cook manageress) and Mrs Gilder.

Neil Ward, ?, ?, Sheila Francis and Eric Bates working with the bees, July 1948.

The school choir, 1955. The photograph includes: Keith Edrich, Cedric Smith, Stephen Rope, Suzanne Nobbs, Jock (Jocelyn) Barrett, Erica Gentle, Margaret Bowring, Anne Galey, Marie Howard, Anthia Rose, Rose Harmer, Marion Cann, Jill Basey-Fisher, Heather Williams, Theresa Gedge, David Trett, Neville London, Mr George (headmaster), Wallace Gowing, Richard Williams, Peter Kippen, Sylvia Kippen, Myra Dye, Cynthia Bickers, Bill Williams, Trevor Trett, Everitt Barnes, Michael Willgress, Geoffrey Wymer, Trevor Macdonald, Clive Griffith, Anne Hardiment, Christine Gilbert, Jean Horner, Pauline Hollis, Angela Clarke, Pat Fuller, Anthea Allen, Susan Penny, Susan Delf, Barbara Basey-Fisher, Barbara Ellis, Sheila Mackerell, Vivienne Buxton, Jean Parker, Jane Jermy, Sandra Spooner, Pat Moore, Enid Warman, Sylvia Barrett.

Staff, 1957. Left to right, back row: *Mr Chase, Miss Goodge, Mr George, Mrs Gilder, Mr Rowarth;* front row: *Mrs Turner, Miss Brown, Mrs Francis, Mrs Luff, Mrs George.*

Miss Josephine Balden's class, 1959.

Many parents worked hard, before and after their normal day's work, to build the swimming pool (below) in 1961.

Sea Lion, *a Mirror dinghy built at the school, was launched at the County Sailing Base at Ludham in 1968.*

At a Festival of Queens at St Andrews Hall, Blofield, in 1963, children presented the £78 they had collected for Sunny Smiles to help needy children. The Queen was Lesley Elson, with attendants Lynda Bates and Jennifer Hipper.

his own goats in an unused thatched cottage by Witton Run bridge and tended bees beside Merrisons Farm in Church Road.

Mr Eric Bacon seemed to have endless energy and enthusiasm for introducing his pupils to a wide range of experiences. From sailing, swimming and music to varied outings, when sometimes large numbers of children went quite far afield, including regular trips abroad.

Active in village life, he also acted as church-

A class with Mr Bacon in 1964. Left to right, back row: Mr Lawrence, Dennis Green, John Green, John Grass, Eric Knowles, Kevin Bussey, Alec Faiers, Colin Edrich, Mr Bacon; middle row: John Bell, John Ellis, Kenneth Hardy, Jane Hare, Gillian Watts, Roy Trett, Stephen Wilkins, Ian Carter; front row: Jennifer Allen, Jane Ringrose, Elizabeth Jermy, Sally Cox, Angela Stanyer, Susan Smithdale, Janet Brown.

Blofield School staff in 1977. Left to right, back row: Mrs McNamara, Mrs Dawe, Miss Chambers, Mrs Cumbers, Mrs McCann; front row: Mrs Middleton, Mr Bacon, Mrs Fraser.

The old woman who lived in a shoe float at the centenary celebrations, 1978.

The netball team, 1979. Left to right, back row: Trudy Kemp, Helen Morley, ?, Jackie King; front row: ?, Bridget Knights, Samantha Byrne.

Juniors in 1979.

Infants in 1979.

Blofield School nativity play in the church, 1979. The photograph includes Michael Johnstone, Amy Rope, Peter North, Karen Bond and Bernice Monck.

Mr and Mrs Howard did crossing patrol duty, followed by Carol Daniels, seen here, in 1982–83.

The recorder group with Mrs Cumbers in 1983. Left to right, back row: Nicholas Rounce, Ross Beales, Paul Auchterlounie, Stuart Feek, Teddy Pritchard, Roger Daniels; middle row: Katherine Blake, Lindsay Clark, Karen Bond, Mrs Cumbers, Annaley Feek, ?, Adam Berry, ?; front row: Heidi Middleton, Amanda Horner, Anne Kinsley, Dawn Hewitt, Hannah Berry, Anna Payne.

Caroline Guyton and Ian Barker learning water safety, 1984. Just seen in the background are Lee Ringwood and Neil Prior.

A trip to Blakeney in May 1984. The picture includes, left to right: Jonathan Pilch, Robert Wood, Paul Auchterlounie, Jason Masala, Jason Rope, Carl Goddard, Adam Hewitt, Katherine Self, Hannah Berry, Dawn Hewitt, Daniel Petley.

Harvest festival in the canteen, October 1984. The photograph includes Gabriel Berry, James Campbell, Timothy Stafford, Carl Smith and Neal Smith.

Miss Todd with the reception class, 1984.

String lessons in 1986. Joanna Willgress is playing the viola.

Staff in 1989. Left to right, back row: *Mrs Prior, Mrs Minden, Mrs Conlin, Mrs Saville, Mrs Harvey;* front row: *Mrs McNamara, Miss Gilbert, Mr Clements, Mr Gleeson, Mrs Cumbers.*

The netball team, 1986. Left to right, back row: *Anna Abramson, Louise Bolangaro;* front row: *Ruth Pilch, Georgina Self, Hayley Patterson, Lucy Conlin, Joanna Blake.*

School leavers in 1989/90. Left to right, back row: *Charlotte Beales, Andrew ?, Selina Baxter, Nicki Balmforth, Stuart Mackerell, Amy Hewitt, Carl Smith;* third row: *Yvette Middleton, Laura Macdonald, John Stafford, Lucy Tetlow, John Weston, Cathy Payne, Emma Williams, Zoe Colman;* second row: *Jessica Walls, Katie Pratt, Robert Sowerby, Mrs Rutter, Sophie Clements, Lucy Pratt, Nicki Gedge;* front row: *Matthew Beales, Corinne Philips, Emma Higton, Ian Cates, Karen Rice, Daniel Briggs, Mark Roberts.*

The school play, c.1990. Left to right, back row: *Helena White, Rebecca Sankey, Amy Rope, Rachel Barber;* front row: *Emily Chambers, Rachel Hardy, Sarah Higton, Amanda Campbell.*

Left: *The football team, 1986.* Left to right, back row: *Teddy Pritchard, Jonathan Bone, Jonathan Watts, Stuart Feek, Neil Prior, Krishan Tatum, James Petley, Mark Payne, Roger Daniels;* front: *Ross Beales, Nicholas Rounce, Ian Wellin, Lee King, Simon Kelf.*

Infants, 2006.

Juniors, 2006.

warden, played the organ and trained the choir.

When he wanted a swimming pool for the school in 1961 County Hall raised difficulties, so he decided to have it built in the schoolhouse garden. Many parents offered their help with expertise, machinery and many hours of hard work.

On its completion an opening ceremony ended with Mr Bacon being thrown into the pool fully clothed, and with Mr Watts pulled into the water whilst helping the headmaster from the pool.

Soon many other schools were visiting to use the pool for their swimming lessons.

There were sailing lessons in the summer holidays, when Mr Bacon taught children at Wroxham Broad in the school's Optimist sailing dinghy. In the summer of 1968 the children who had instruction included Ruth Horne, Vanessa Kemp, Louise Stramik, Stephen Gladwin, Lynne Buxton, Sally Matthews and Sandra Bullen.

A wide variety of musical instruments were on loan, there were lessons in school, orchestras to join and school choirs performed locally and in Norwich.

Hemblington School

Dolly Bailey, born in 1900, was a scholar, a pupil teacher and then a teacher at Hemblington School. She retired from teaching in 1960. Her mother died in 1966 and, sadly, Dolly herself died the same year.

Roy Jermy's first teacher in the infants' class was Miss Dolly Bailey:

She was a kind lady with a lot of patience. She lived with her mother, who kept a general shop not far from the school. We used to call in on the way home at her mother's shop, when we had sufficient money, to buy a few sweets. She used to have rows of tall jars of various sweets of different colours and flavours.

Hemblington School, c.1925. Front row: *Tommy Knights* (fifth from left), *Ernie Barnes* (seventh), *Douglas Bailey* (eighth).

Miss Bailey's class, 1935. Left to right, back row: *Miss Bailey, Clive Waterson, Jim Tyrell, Leslie Griffin, Henry Ling, Robin Pope, Kenneth Carter, Donny Babbington;* middle row: *Doris Newstead, Gracie Payne, Eric Dawson, Ronnie Dawson, Gordon Thrower, Derek Harper, Hazel Norton, Jean Brookfield;* front row: *Nancy Skedge, Rene Houghton, Betty Jermy, Mona Griffin, Dolly Griffin, Doris Buckland, Christine Harper, Myrtle Waterson.*

Infant class, c.1919. Left to right, back row: *Dolly Bailey, Leslie Hylton, ?, ?, ?, George Parker, Charlie Hubbard, ?, ?, Milly Whittaker, Arthur Browne;* third row: *? Parker, ?, Leonard 'Dan' Hubbard, ?, ?, ?, ?, George Townsend;* second row: *Jessie Manners, ?, ?, ?, ?, ?, Hilda Griffin;* front row: *?, ?, Ivy Whittaker (later Ryan).*

I remember at the end of each day at school in the infant class we used to sing 'Now the day is over, night is drawing nigh, shadows of the evening steal across the sky', and we used to sing it with such gusto as we knew it was the end of the day and we would be on our way home.

My next class teacher was Miss Alice Jordan. She lived several miles from the school in a village called Surlingham which is the other side of the River Yare from Brundall. She lodged with Miss Bailey during the week and cycled home after school on Fridays.

Mrs Mildred Snelling, who taught the next class, was also a kind lady.

The final year at school was in the Headmaster's class. His name was Donald Babbington and he lived in the School House adjoining the school. He was a very kind man who was also very well built so we had to behave ourselves!

We always had a large Christmas tree given at Christmas time by Major Harker of Blofield Hall. We were asked to write our names on a slip of paper saying what present we would like. I remember I always used to ask for a torch.

Roy Snelling asked for something rather unusual. One Christmas there was to be a school party with a

The 1930 netball team's cup was given by the Harkers. Left to right, back row: *Mr Parvin (headmaster), Vera Chipperfield (later Hylton), Norah Graver (later Moss), Ruby Alderton, Edie Waterson, Miss Pegg;* front row: *Molly Parvin, Betty Stapleton, Violet Hubbard (later Wicks).*

present under the tree for every child. Roy went round Woolworths to choose his present. He was allowed 6d. Seeing some electrical flex, he worked out how much he could get and put in an application for three yards of flex. His mother, who was teaching at the same school, said that the master, Mr Babbington, wouldn't allow it because it was too dangerous, so they gave him something else. Roy explains:

Well I did procure some wire. They were just putting electricity into the villages. Until then it was just candles to bed and an oil-lamp to read by. My grandmother lived opposite. I couldn't do any experiments at

Children dressed as members of a band for a school concert, c.1931. Left to right: Arthur Jermy, Basil Shreeve, Doris Knights, Peggy Thrower, Dennis Buckland, Beryl Stapleton, Maisie Alden, Alec Barber, Roy Jermy and Edwin Dunch.

An 'oven in the wall' in the schoolhouse in the 1950s.

The drinking water pump in the schoolhouse garden, 1950s. The name of the boy is unknown.

A cycle outing for 14 and 15 year olds, 1950s. Eric Smith can be seen at the centre in a cap.

Enid Stanbrook with the new wash basin in the 1950s.

A trip to the Festival of Britain in London on 27 May 1951. At the back: Mrs Waterson (in hat) and Janet Frankland (beside her); in front: Graham Martin, Eric Cooper, Brian Francis, Margaret Rope, David Griffin, ? Stevens, Catherine Chipperfield.

Miss Bailey with her class of infants in 1952. Left to right at left hand table: Jean Palgrave, Carol Webb, Margaret Griffin, Clifford Francis, Anita Tilney, Jean Frankland, Alan Griffin, Jean Snelling, Joan Griffin; at tables on right (front): Enid Watson, John Frankland, ? Burdett, Valerie Wright; behind: Jacqueline Bowring, Molly Knights, ?; sitting on floor: Stephen Holmes, David Knights and Christopher Palgrave.

Building a stack of hay from the playing-field for feeding the goats in the winter, 1953. The children also built a goat house using timber and reeds, covered with wire netting so the reeds were not eaten.

The senior class with Mr Watson, 1952. Tables on left, back to front: David Carter and David Griffin, Gloria Jermy and Margaret Rope, Colin Andrews and Brian Francis; tables on right, back to front: Katherine Brown and Janet Frankland, Graham Martin and Mig Jones, Wendy Havis and Margaret Smithdale, Hilary Starkings and Desmond Tilney, Rodney Holmes and ?.

Staff in 1954. Left to right, back row: Mr Watson, Mr Chase; front: ?, ?, Miss Bailey, ?.

Left: The school goat project, 1953. The school's nanny goat had two kids which the children are weighing. Left to right: Kathleen Brown, Janet Frankland, Colin Andrews, Margaret Rope.

A production of Captain Noah and his Floating Zoo, *July 1977.* Pictured are: *Andrew Poyle, Mark Pitman, Joanne Filby, Becky Wildman, Neil Smith, Gary Finley, Sarah Cook, Tracy Bartle, Belinda Selbie, Sharon Bland, Suzie Kendall, Michelle Burton, Robert Snelling, Dominique Nicholson, Samantha Colman, Sarah George, Sarah Mindham, Marie Debbage, Nina Hill, Maria Chryssafi, Sally McLaughlin, Karen Batchelor, Stephanie Purdy, David Griffith, Nicola Lewis, Paula Webb, Emma Willshire, Andrew Kirkby, Melanie March, Katie Elcocks, Jane Ingram, Katie Seymore.*

Craft display, July 1978. Standing at left, left to right: Kevin Daines, Anthony Kiernan, Julian Green, Chris Chryssafi, Simon Youngs, Timothy Wildman, Paul Green, Neil Smith; standing on right: John East, Andrew Byatt, Shaun King, Kevin Francis, Karl Andrews, Alan Hale; at front: Simon Foster, Simon Lewis, Mark Genery, Stephen Cooper, John Hamlin, Kevin Bingham, Tom Stephens, James Batchelor.

Centenary display of girls' needlework, July 1978. **Left to right:** *Melanie March, Sarah Hamlin, Nicola Lewis, ?, Joanne Alby, Linda Bedson, Katie Elcocks, Samantha Colman, Stephanie Purdy, Sally McLaughlin, Marika Chryssafi, Susan Griffin, Lucy Foster.*

Easter bulb growing competition, 1972. **Left to right:** *Linda Bedson, ?, Robert Snelling, ?, ?, Alan Hale, Dawn Batchelor, Elizabeth Morgan, ?, Mark Burton, ?, Jacquie Chapman, Matthew Morgan, Susan Bell, Susan Griffin, ?, ?.*

Above: Man from Galilee, *with Blair Law, Darren Webb, Mark Francis, Marcus English, Mark Cook, Peter Hornsby, Helen Ball, Joanna Burleigh, Andrew Shreeve, Carol Colthurst, Jack Stevens, Sarah Gilbert, Jenny Jones, Matthew Bates, Stephen Yaxley, Julian Millar, Kim English, Jonathan Nortcliffe, Samantha Triggs, Karl Francis, Damien Mitchell, James Norton, James Ong, Justin Norton, Michael Aldridge, Nicola McKay, Neil Oxberry, Joanne Bucknell, Marianne Purdy, Matthew Darley, Carole Brooks, Sarah Bussey, Jason Stangroom, David Huggins, Elizabeth Rose, Victoria Turner, Tim Stock, Martin Howes, Susan Gedge, Isobel Ong, Helen Bates, Shelley Pond, Sarah Hemmings, Marika Chryssafi, Marsha King, Stefan Gosling, Alisdair Marks, Tanya Rant, Christopher Riley, Claire March, Elliott Pascoe-Stevens, Caroline Chryssafi, Julie Bussey.*

Alice Brown, 1941. She left school at 14 and worked as a clippie on Norwich buses.

home; my father was very tight on discipline, thankfully. So I went to my grandmother's with my piece of wire and I pushed it into a socket. There was a loud bang, crash and all the lights went out and I was petrified. If my father knew of that just what would he do? So I went to Mr Fleming over the road, who came and repaired the fuse and all was well. That was my introduction to electricity, a loud bang!

Some had a long walk

When Arthur Browne was six years old he went to stay with his grandmother at Panxworth. He had to walk over two field paths to Pedham and thence to school.

Phyllis Jermy, who went to live at South Walsham when she was seven, still attended Hemblington School:

I walked all that way, a seven year old across two fields and right round to Hemblington Hall Road and up to school, then home again. We wouldn't do it now would we?

Infants, 2005.

Juniors, 2005.

Alice Brown:

I liked school; it was a happy time. In the 1930s the headmaster was Parvin and then we had Babbington. He moved to Mulbarton. He recognised me on the Mulbarton bus. He was very nice. Parvin used to tan the girls. The big boys would play tricks on that governor. There was only one playground, no field to play on. Over the fence there was a field of strawberries. I went through after some. I walked from Blofield Corner to school four times a day, home to dinner and back again. There weren't any dinners then. We had our dinner when my father came home.

I passed my scholarship and I should have gone as a pupil teacher but as the oldest my mother couldn't afford it. So I had to take what I could get, which was working on the buses.

We moved into Blofield when I was 13 but I still walked to Hemblington because I liked the master. There was a thunderstorm one afternoon. I was a bit frightened and I was soaking wet when I got home. I was afraid of thunderstorms till I went on the buses in Norwich and the bombs came. I was never afraid of thunder again.

Head teachers at Hemblington

Miss Walker, 1878	Mr G. Chase, 1956
Mr Deeks, 1882	Mr G. King, 1956
Mr Powlson, 1904	Mrs Tucker, 1964
Mr Foreman, 1906	Mr P. Hamlin, 1969
Mr Leonard Parvin, 1919	Mr M. Webb, 1985
Mr A. Babbington, 1931	Mr Stephen Bloor, 1986
Mr Watson, 1943	Mr Chris Cannell, 1994
Mr J. Hewitt, 1956	Mrs Catherine Ansett, 2001

CHAPTER 3

Churches and Chapels

All Saints Church at Hemblington

The church of Hemblington stands in solitary state on high ground in a corner of the parish. It is fourteenth century, with an earlier round tower.

Although the medieval village of Hemblington was originally close by, to the east of the church, it is thought to have been abandoned during the seventeenth century when plague struck and the villagers moved to new homes a little distance away at Pedham.

The earliest feature of the building is its circular tower, assigned to 'the Saxo-Norman period', roughly between 1060 and 1100. A small slab of Barnack stone pierced with a circular hole about six inches in diameter, now blocked up, was evidently intended to serve as a look-out for some purpose.

Many towers, now attached to churches, were built for defensive purposes, necessary on the East Coast in pre-Norman days.

Amongst the stone and flint of the church construction are fragments of Roman tile, their terracotta showing mellow tones.

Reusing material is clearly nothing new – a stone coffin lid has been used as a step and some of the roof timbers show traces of prior use. In former times the roof was part lead and part thatch.

The font is of great interest. It is eight-sided and beautifully decorated with a host of saintly figures, eight on the stem, with the Holy Trinity and seven more saints in the rich carving of the bowl.

The quality of the font and the large wall painting reflect the wealth used to help create and furnish this lovely, unique church.

The mural paintings

In 1937, when many thicknesses of whitewash were removed from the walls of the nave, important medieval paintings were revealed.

The subject is the legend of St Christopher, with

View of Hemblington Church, 1967.

Roman tiles built in amongst the flint, identified by the late Keith Darby, diocesan and cathedral architect.

The Holy Trinity and 15 saintly figures are shown on the font.

The mural of St Christopher.

details of his early life as Reprobus, a huge heathen giant whose one wish was to serve the strongest man in the world. He is pictured, supported by his staff, carrying the Christ Child on his shoulder.

Church records
Before the Norman Conquest in 1066, Ailmar, Bishop of Elmham, had land in this parish.

From 1716 onwards many instances of the Jary and Heath families appear in the registers, and in 1734 the constable's accounts show a sum of 1s. for mending the town gate, and a sum of 3d., paid to Edward Heath, for 'an eye for ye town gate'.

Bishop Blomfield, Bishop of London 1828–56, took a wife from the household of Hemblington Hall.

The Weston family has had a long association with Hemblington Church, beginning when Nathaniel Weston moved into nearby Gables Farm in 1834 and became churchwarden in 1852.

At this time the church was in debt and he took it upon himself to pay the church expenses out of his own pocket.

Nat's great nephew, Godfrey (1875–1923), took over both the farm and the post of churchwarden and it was he who saved the church from demolition when he secured its restoration after the roof was blown off in a great gale.

In March 1895 it was reported in the deanery magazine that:

The hurricane was at its height while the congregation were in the church. The nave roof and that of the porch suffered and owing to the dangerous state of the roof the service was somewhat shortened and the people dismissed without a sermon. A large tree fell in the churchyard during the service but, providentially, just escaped the church.

In 1898 the Bishop of Norwich spoke out for 'your little Church at Hemblington which I can testify needs restoration sorely.' He thought the parishioners had come forward 'right well' with funds. 'A church rescued from neglect and restored to seemliness and good order is usually followed (Deo

Gratias) by a higher spiritual life in the parish.'

Godfrey's son, also Godfrey and a churchwarden, continued the family farming tradition at Gables Farm and it was he who, aged 86 and still churchwarden, inspired a second restoration in 1968. He renewed the roof, restored the porch and repointed the tower. It was only at this time that Hemblington Church finally had electric lighting and heating installed, as part of major restoration works. Until then, oil-lamps were the only source of light.

Hemblington Church was served by a series of curates until 1925. Since then one rector has looked after both parishes

Churchwardens
Many have served as churchwarden – initially, one was chosen for the people and one as the rector's warden. Nowadays there is no such distinction. At the time of writing the churchwardens are Mary Darby and Simon Mutten at Hemblington and Jim Morley and Bryan Jenkins at Blofield.

Rectors at Blofield
1608	Edmund Suckling
1628	Richard Baldwin
1634	Ambrose Congham
1646	Alexander Shipdham
1654	Samuel Maltby
1671	Charles Reve
1727	James Dover
1735	Philip Candler
1769	James Carlos
1804	John Drew Borton
1847	Thomas Smith Turnbull
1876	John Lamb
1880	James Percy Garrick
1912	Arthur Duncan Jones
1915	Arthur Shillito
1947	Henry Kingsley Percival Smith
1956	Robert Spencer Canning Baily
1970	Nicholas Scarth Dixon
1978	Albert George Baker

Since the temporary suspension of the patronage in 1995 we have had a priest-in-charge.
1995	Peter Thorn
2000	Philip Unsworth

Recent Rectors of Blofield and Hemblington

Canon Garrick served on the board of the village schools, knew his parishioners and was liked by them. He retired in 1912, and on his death it was reported in the 1919 deanery magazine that: 'One who knew him well wrote that he never knew him say an unkind word, or complain of his loss of sight which meant so much to him.'

The Revd Duncan Jones was at Blofield for only three years. At Cambridge he had become junior

The Revd Percival Smith with bride and groom, 1955.
Left to right: Roy Debbage, John Cushion, David Poll,
Revd Percival Smith, Doreen Poll (née Harper), John
Howard, John Debbage.

Arthur Duncan Jones with Blofield Scouts in 1914.

Arthur and Ellen Shillito's wedding, 1922.

dean at a young age, and when he left Blofield in 1915 he went on to be Dean of Chichester and then Exeter.

Canon Arthur Shillito was highly esteemed as a musician. His writing in deanery magazines has provided a social history document of contemporary events with perceptive comments.

A kind man, many people remember that he baptised them, prepared them for confirmation and married them. Baden and Evelyn Hanton well remember him marrying them in 1944.

Arthur and Ellen Shillito received a gift from the parishes on their 25th wedding anniversary in 1947 and decided to put the £63.10s. towards buying a motor car, which became known as the rectory car!

Older residents remember going to the rectory to pay into shoe and clothing clubs and receiving a kind welcome from Mrs Shillito. Twopence a week could be paid into the Sunday-school shoe club towards the cost of new footwear and the Turnbull Charity added threepence in the pound to deposits drawn at the end of the year. Clothing club cards could be used at Frank Price's shop in Magdalen Street.

Gwen Shillito, her daughter, led the cubs and, before the war, held a small kindergarten school in rooms at the back of the rectory.

Children often attended both church and chapel, enjoying the outings and parties of both, of course!

At the turn of the nineteenth century, when Canon Garrick was rector, the treat was held during the first week of the summer holidays on the rectory lawn. One of the children, in their old age, wrote this account:

The children assembled at 2p.m. and all was in readi-
ness. A large swing had been fixed to the chestnut tree
on the lawn bordering the Church Alley. Various old
games were played on the lawn in front of the house,
including 'Here we come gathering nuts and may' and
'In and out the windows'. Skipping ropes were in full
swing and races took place on the lawn.

But the great event was the tea, and three long tres-
tles had been arranged on the lawn facing the front door,
laden with good things, all prepared in the morning by
willing hands who came to the parish room in the
Rectory to prepare the tea. Big urns stood on the tables
and tea was in great demand.

More games followed tea and at about 9p.m. Canon
Garrick stood by the gate leading from the front to the
back lawn and stables. As each child passed through the
gate Canon Garrick gave them a large packet of sweets
and a few erring souls were known to run quickly round
the house and again join the end of the queue! But as
the Canon had poor sight this passed unnoticed.

When evening shadows began to fall Canon Garrick
gathered the children around him on the lawn and sent
up dozens of coloured balloons. This brought the
happy day to a close and the children departed, very
happy and contented, after a day of simple pleasures
and happiness.

The path from village to church
Formerly, a cornfield stretched from the church right to the top of Blofield Street.

Running across the fields from the village was a path which used to be called 'Church Way' or the 'Old Bowling Green Alley' and is now named Church Alley.

Keith Beck and his daughter Laura walking down Church Alley to her wedding, 2005.

An early view of the rectory. Note the caged crinoline dresses, worn in fashionable circles until 1856, but still worn in the country after that date.

Pony and trap at The Cedars, 1920s.

Along its length lanterns were fixed to the trees to light the way to evening services. The fixing for one of these can still be seen embedded in the trunk of a tree.

At the church end of the path are granite gateposts which most likely were brought as ballast on the Scottish fishing boats which came down the East Coast in pursuit of the herring shoals. The sale of such items earned the skipper some extra income.

It was only after the First World War that part of this area was purchased as a war memorial and fields became a village recreation ground.

Where the incumbents lived
The rectory to the east of the church, in what used to be called Church Gate Street (now known as Church Road), was demolished about 1806 and rebuilt on the north side of the road. Many of the bricks from the former house were used in building the 'new' rectory.

From 1806 to 1950 this rectory was home to John Borton, Thomas Turnbull, John Lamb, James Garrick, Arthur Duncan Jones, Arthur Shillito and Henry Percival Smith respectively. In 1952 Mr C.E. Kevill-Davies, director of Lacons Brewery, purchased the rectory from the church commissioners for £3,000 and the house was renamed the Old Hall.

In 1950 the Revd Percival Smith moved to the house now known as The Cedars, on the Yarmouth Road opposite the Margaret Harker Hall.

In Stocks Lane the house known as Lilburnes (later named Ferniehill), was inhabited in 1885 by the Misses Coleman and was at that time the only house between the King's Head and Bay Bridge Farm. Ferniehill became the rectory, the Revd Robert Canning Baily moving there in 1966.

In July 1987 the Revd Albert Baker moved from Stocks Lane to the newly built house The Rectory in Oak Wood.

St Andrew and St Peter's Church, Blofield

This church has seen worshippers entering its doors for nearly 600 years. The worn step tells of the many feet that have come into this place for so many different reasons.

When the bishop performed the act of consecrating the building in 1427 he anointed various places on the walls with holy oil and made the sign of the cross. Some of these were later painted or carved.

The medieval font was originally quite colourful. Unusually, it has scenes from the life of Christ around the bowl, and these and the Tudor roses around the stem and the heads and shields under the bowl were painted. In a few areas traces of the original colours can still be seen.

Canon Garrick wrote that the church:

... stands on the summit of rising ground, sloping upwards from the meadows below. The churchyard is a

Canon Garrick, 1885.

Blofield Church from the meadows to the south, c.1910.

Mr Beverley with the replacement stone figure he carved for Blofield's church tower in 1965.

picturesque and pleasant spot; flanked on the north by a row of fine lime trees, carpeted in the spring with prim-roses and daffodils and a host of wildflowers preserved in ancient ground it seems an ideal resting place for the faithful dead.

Arthur Mee wrote of the late-fourteenth-century church, whose magnificent tower is a landmark in the countryside: 'The church possesses a noble tower, 110 feet high.' From the top one can see as far as Norwich Cathedral to the west and Happisburgh lighthouse at the coast.

Canon Garrick praised the fine flint work in the tower and mentioned the four figures which surmount the parapet. These same figures have caused some problems, and it took a while to replace one of the kings in 1605. The archdeacon pronounced that:

One of the Kinges made of freestone being an ornament to the steeple being blown down two years past is not yet set up again which is a great blemish and defacing of the good steeple.

In 1964 the 'kingly figure' at the north west of the parapet was struck by lightning only minutes after the conclusion of the Sunday morning service.

A Norwich sculptor, Mr Beverley, had previously worked on the restoration of the Ethelbert Gate of Norwich Cathedral. He used a half-ton block of Ancaster stone to carve a 4½ foot tall replacement for the figure missing from Blofield's tower. Said to be an evangelist, it is robed and heavily bearded and holds a staff which terminates in a cross. 'The orig-inal figure dated from the 15th century and was too badly damaged to copy,' said Mr Beverley.

Storm damage reported in the deanery magazine March 1895 in Blofield:

The lead roofing in the nave was completely torn off and the cross on the roof of the chancel was blown down. It was a solid stone cross, 5 feet across and weighing at least two hundredweight. Many large trees in the meadows were uprooted but the avenue of lime trees was untouched. This had been planted in 1820 by William Codling when he was master at Reve's school.

Evensong was at 3p.m. and soon after the commence-ment Canon Garrick decided to stop and to clear the church which he felt sure to be unsafe. The noise of the wind is said to have been terrific. On leaving the church, many people were blown right across to the east end of the churchyard.

The wind attained the force of a hurricane and was more violent and destructive than anything experienced within the memory of living men.

Bells: a call to worship

The church has a fine peal of bells. Bellringer Aubrey Forster tells their story:

In 1552 King Edward VI sent commissioners to all 690 churches in Norfolk to produce inventories of church goods, which included the bells. Blofield was one of the few churches which had five bells, with the largest (a tenor) weighing in at 18 hundredweight.

In 1819 the bells were rehung by Samuel Thurston and were officially opened by five St Peter Mancroft ringers.

The five bells are named:

'Anno Domini 1581 (John Brend Snr)'.

'John Brend Made Me 1656'.

'Elias Brend Made Me 1660'. This is a rare bell as only 20 of the Elias Brend bells remain in Norfolk.

'En Multis Annis Resonet Campana Eohts'. (Let John's bell ring out for many years).

The tenor declares 'John Stephens Made Me 1719'.

In 1826 a treble bell was added by T.J. Hurry. The bells were opened in 'grand style' and in 1827 12 pairs

The rededication of bells in 1962 after seven years' silence. Standing on extreme left at the back is Cecil Sharman and the verger in black is Ben Hanton.

Celebrating the dedication of two treble bells, 1980. Left to right: Judy Frostwick, Jim Morley, Neil Thomas, Helen Fowler, Richard Morley, Bishop Blackburne, Ian Tilney, Helen Grass, Kenny Frostwick, Revd Albert Baker, Anthea Morley.

Feb. 22nd. 1827

Was rung in this Steeple seven hundred and 20 changes, of Grandsire Bob, in 3 hours and 20 minutes, the Peals conducted by JAMES. HURRY. and rung by the under mentioned Names.

JAMES. HURRY. Treble.

JOSEPH. HARMAN. 2nd.

ADAM. DUNT. 3rd.

JOSHUA. HURRY. 4th.

WILLᴹ. STOCKENS. 5th.

JOSEPH. E. BANE. Tenor.

Mᴿ. JAMES. BROWNE.

Churchwarden, many Years, a lover of the science expresst his high approbation of the above Performance.

A plaque in the ringing chamber commemorating the bell-ringing contest.

of gloves were presented at the Globe Inn to the two companies of ringers who rang the best 720 changes.

Unfortunately the bells became difficult to ring as they were hung high up in the tower and the plain bearings that supported them became very worn. In 1962 they were rehung by Whitechapel of London in a new steel 'H' frame for eight bells lower in the tower. A new ringing gallery was also built. The bells were rededicated by Archdeacon Henry Percival Smith, former rector of Blofield.

Two treble bells were added in 1980, making Blofield a full octave of eight bells. These bells were cast from two bells used in the, by now redundant, Church of St Mary in Thetford.

An additional chiming bell, cast at Whitechapel, was added in June 2003 in memory of Roy and Marjorie Granger.

Captain unable to ring... leg crushed by tree!
Randall Ward, captain of the ringers was unable to take part when a muffled peal was rung as a tribute to those who had fallen in action during 1915. Unfortunately in clearing away a tree blown down by the gale on Boxing Day, he had his leg crushed by a very heavy portion of the trunk.

Windows in memory of those who have worshipped here
The Garden window is in memory of Frank Neave, who lived for a time in the Rookery in Church Road. A farmer and botanist, he produced several new varieties of flower, some illustrated in the three gardens of Eden, Resurrection and Gethsemane.

The dedication of a chiming bell in memory of Roy and Marjorie Granger in 2003, with the Revd Philip Unsworth and churchwardens Jim Morley and Rosemary Hammond.

The Kempe window of 1922 pictures three soldier saints; St Alban, St George and St Martin. This was given by his father, Dr Anderson, in memory of Kenneth Anderson, a young man killed in the First World War in France. His grandmother, a member of the Tuck family, had lived in Blofield.

The Margaret Harker memorial windows depict her activities, interests and generosity to the parish. These include running a war hospital in Brundall House from 1914 to 1916; her Red Cross work, including care of the Scottish fisher girls, and her love of children, which prompted her inauguration of an infant welfare centre in the village.

The West window was given in 1927 in memory of Mrs Pells of the Cedars. It shows St Felix the Evangelist of East Anglia, St Edmund King and Martyr, St Christopher with a shrine and church and Bishop Percy, who died at his palace in Blofield in 1369. Also depicted are coats of arms, including those of Caius College, Cambridge, patrons of the church.

A window given in 1878 in memory of the Tuck family has been rescued from obscurity behind the organ and placed above the consecration cross in the north aisle. It was rededicated by the archdeacon of Norfolk, the Venerable David Hayden on 27 November 2005.

In the main east window Sir Peter Eade's life is commemorated.

Worship in the nineteenth century
From the autobiography of Sir Peter Eade of Blofield, 1825–1915.

The church services were on Sunday morning and afternoon only and there was no curate; though, some years later, the rector did engage such an assistant.

At this time there were no regular church collections but at intervals of about three months a 'Charity Sermon' was preached, and a collection made for one of the principal religious societies. This was quite an event and I remember how, on these occasions, a formal letter from the Bishop was read, always ending with a request in the same words, that the preacher would 'effectually incite his congregation to a liberal contribution.'

Worship through music
Peter Eade wrote:

At the end of the eighteenth century the north and south aisles had tall pews for the families of the 'better classes'. The reputed quality of the 'owners' of these pews began at the top of the aisle and gradually diminished downwards to its lowest part where many of the gentlemen's servants sat. The nave was fitted with rows of open benches allocated to poor women of the parish on the right of the central aisle and the poor men on the left. Below the reading desk was a sturdy pew for the parish clerk, Mr William Codling, who read the responses out very audibly, gave out the hymns and loudly said the amens. As there was no organ or harmonium the initial note of hymns was usually given by a clarinet.

From early years music formed an important part of church life. In 1848 the Revd Turnbull bought a

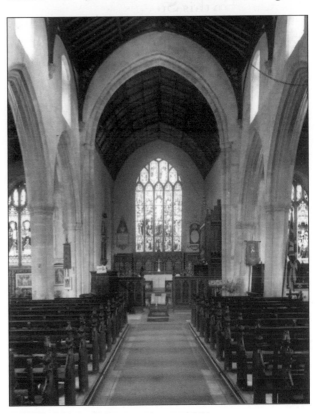

The organ was in the chancel until the 1950s.

barrel organ for the church. It had two barrels with ten tunes on each, so the variety of weekly worship must have been rather restricted. On one occasion the mechanism stuck and it played its entire repertoire without pause.

This was replaced in 1866 by a small organ placed at the west end of the church. It was customary to turn, when singing, to face the organ. It seems that ladies wearing crinoline dresses tended to get stuck half way round in the restricted space between the pews!

The organists at Blofield Church included Miss Ruth Ainsworth, 1932; Eric Bacon, 1962; Sydney Lee, 1970; Geoff Sankey, 1998; James Henderson, 2001. Removed from a redundant church in Upper Holloway, London, the present Hill organ was completely overhauled and dedicated with a concert in June 1999.

The choir at Blofield Church was once 40 strong and outings were enjoyed by all. From the deanery magazine, 20 July 1907:

An excursion of the choir, kindly organised by Mr and Mrs Rix, took place on the Bure today. The party, going partly by rail, and partly by road, met at Acle bridge, where they found a steam launch and a motor boat by which they proceeded to Benet Abbey where they had lunch and went afterwards as far as Horning where they had tea… Many thanks to Mr Rix for initiating and organising the trip and securing an admirable supply of abundant provisions that none should faint by the way.

Many boys sang in the choir and some have their names on the board which records Chamberlin prizewinners from 1923 to 1967:

Graver, Sharman, Beck, Pardon, Bickers, Williams, Gedge, Edrich, Trett, Simmons, Horner, Ribbons, Allen, Marshall, Dunham, Merrison, Palgrave, Foulger, Knights, Mackerell, Debbage, Betts, Rope, Gibbs, White, Cushion, Hague, Poll, Gardiner, Turner, Gilder,

Moore, Fuller, Howard, Baynes, Brigham, Stone, Taylor, Willgress, Baily, Dawson, Smellie, Oliver, Farrell, Athow, Bacon.

In those times nearly all boys attended church or chapel and they tell stories of the pranks and fun they enjoyed. Mr Browne, who pumped the organ, used to reprimand them. If they talked during the sermon, 'You got a hymnal rapped over your head.' Others confess to having scratched their names behind the organ when taking their turn to pump the bellows.

John Howard had a fine voice. He remembers winning the Chamberlin prize, which was worth £3, £2 and £1 for coming first, second or third. He was proud to go to the cathedral each year. He remembers that Dr Heathcote Statham tested the choirboys

The choir at St Benet's Abbey, c.1956. Left to right, back row: Revd Canning Baily, John Debbage, Mrs George, Roy Debbage, Douglas Dawson, Cecil Sharman; front row: Canning Baily junr, Malcolm Jones, Geoff Wymer, Kenneth Horner.

Sydney and Mary Lee's retirement party, 1998. Left to right, back row: Sydney Lee, Joyce Willgress, Mary Lee, Gladys Jermany; in front: Percy Pardon.

A double wedding, 4 July 1953. Left to right: Grahame Baynes, ? Dale, Roy Debbage, David Taylor, John Cushion, Brian Claxton, Margaret Rose Claxton (née Bates), Sidney Critoph, Marjorie Alice Critoph (née Bates), Eric Forster, John Debbage, Aubrey Forster, John Howard, ?, Eddie Willimott.

Hemblington Church choir, c.1935. Left to right, back row: *Arthur Thrower, Tom Wright, Freda Rix, Peggy Smith, Doris Thrower;* middle row: *Arthur Jermy, Edwin Dunch, George Townsend, Roy Jermy, Eric Waterson;* front row: *Doris Knights, Hazel Newstead, Sylvia Carter, Hazel Jermy, Sheila Harvey.*

each year. Miss Ainsworth was choir mistress and Friday night was practice night.

A task remembered by one head choirboy was that of climbing the tower to raise the Union Jack.

Mr Cecil Sharman sang in the church choir from the time he was 11 until he was 70, winning the first prize several times. His widow Muriel recalls, 'He had a voice like Ernest Luff. When his voice broke he sang baritone but, when the choir was short of tenors, he could sing tenor.'

At Hemblington Mrs Rix was organist and choir teacher. Young members of the choir attended practices in the front room of her cottage after school. Roy Jermy thinks they were paid 4d. for each practice! Tom Wright used to carry the cross at church services, doing his best to avoid hitting the hanging oil-lamps.

John Bulley was another choir member. He recalls Canon Shillito, a nice man:

He used to come round when we had choir practice in Mrs Rix's house on Mill Road. He'd listen to us and he used to say, don't sing 'yah-ah-ah-ah-ah, go coo-oo-oo-oo-oo.'

Roy Batchelor remembers that at the end of the war, in 1945 or '46, when a 'Songs of Praise' service was broadcast from Blofield Church, the wires had to run all the way from the telephone exchange in Brundall. The last of the Royal Engineers, before they left after the war, took the wires along the pavement right down Highfield Avenue and along to the church. Billy Merrison was linesman in charge and it was a long, tiring job going to and fro.

He walked into the exchange on Saturday afternoon and they asked him, 'What's wrong, Billy?' 'Nothing's wrong,' he said, 'but I think it's time to put the kettle on; it's a long way back from Blofield to Brundall.'

Globe Lane Chapel

A mission room and Sunday school in Globe Lane opened in 1889. Miss Alice Amelia Cameron owned it and she and her sister, Miss Octavia Louisa Heath Jary, were the trustees. In 1911, they provided a manse.

Many remember enjoying exciting children's activities here, with games on the chapel field. From the school log-book, 1979:

School service for leavers held in canteen. Mr Harry Hammond of the Blofield Free Anglican Church officiated and gave an inspiring address in which he compared life 50 years ago when he was a pupil at

The Mission Hall, Globe Lane, 1906.

41

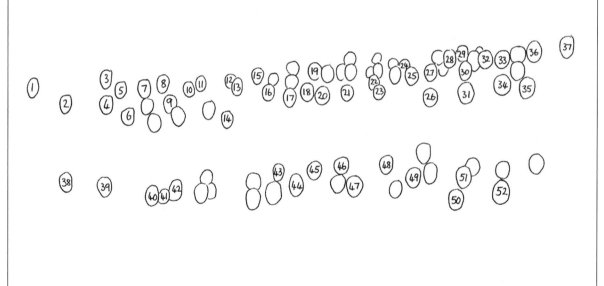

A gathering at Globe Lane Chapel, c.1942. Those present have been identified by Betty Bates. 1. Mr Turner, 2. Jimmy Alden, 3. Albert Nobbs, 4. Tony White, 5. Edna Snelson, 6. Barbara Roat, 7. Miriam Basey, 8. Sibyl Nobbs, 9. David Allen, 10. Valerie Gedge, 11. Mrs Stanley Gedge, 12. Mrs Hazel, 13. Peter Street, 14. Margery Bates, 15. Mrs Martins, 16. Roger Allen, 17. Donald Cushion, 18. Gerald Allen, 19. Mrs Doris Poll, 20. John Gilder, 21. David Poll, 22. Nigel Poll, 23. Harry Knights, 24. Mrs Spanton, 25. Betty Barber, 26. Chris Barrett, 27. Ruth Ford, 28. Molly Rose, 29. Mrs Rose, 30. John Alden, 31. Chris Basey, 32. Betty Rose, 33. Mr Hazel, 34. John Bailey, 35. Neville Allen, 36. Doreen Fox, 37. Mr Harry Smith, 38. Roy Cann, 39. Hazel Moss, 40. Gillian Rope, 41. Michael Gilder, 42. Peter Gilder, 43. Jenifer Poll, 44. Eric Bates, 45. Peggy Hanton, 46. Margaret Barrett, 47. Glenna Rope, 48. Margaret Bates, 49. ? Fox, 50. Marion Gedge, 51. Joan Francis, 52. Jacqueline Gedge.

Blofield Heath Methodist Chapel in 2006.

Blofield, with that of school children today & all that is done for them.

Barry Raven had been on the Methodist circuit for some years before coming to Globe Lane as pastor in 1983 with his wife Andrée and children Caroline, Matthew and Alison.

The chapel now has electric lighting, toilet and kitchen facilities, making it a welcoming meeting-place.

Blofield Heath Methodist Chapel

Blofield Health Methodist Chapel was built in 1868 as a Primitive Methodist chapel. The present pews came from Calvert Street chapel when it closed in 1966. The original box pulpit has been replaced by a platform.

A Sunday school began in 1883. By 1977 the number of children attending was 40 and a school-room was built beside the chapel. In the 1990s a very successful Shipmates Group for children met midweek. At the time of writing the chapel is working on 'Village Methodists of the 21st century, the way forward.' Alan Wakeman is the minister.

Charlie Howes lived in Blofield from 1929, apart for a few years in the war, until his retirement in 1988.

He attended Sunday school at the chapel throughout his childhood and then the head and second stewards, Mr Futter and Mr Stapleton, persuaded him to take on the stewardship role.

Years went by and Mr Watson, who arrived as carpentry master at Blofield School, also attended chapel. When he became headmaster at Hemblington School he became even more involved, becoming the chapel's Sunday-school superintendent.

Charlie and his sisters were involved in all the anniversaries, at which the children memorised and gave recitations. Mr Watson was treasurer and, when

A charabanc outing from the Cuttons Corner chapel in 1925. The photograph includes (left to right at the back): Stanley Neve, Billy Barnes, Leonard Hubbard, Mr Chamberlin's son, Arthur Browne, Ernest Barnes, Ruby Barber, George Brown, Tommy Knights, Mr Chamberlin (a preacher); at the front: Kenny Hylton, Douglas Rogers (with a stick), Mr Self (a preacher), Maidy Webb, Mary Kahler, Aggie Hall, Mr Self's daughter, Rosie Merrison, ? Sutton, May Marjoram, Winnie Bulley, Evelyn Evans, Vera Hylton, Mrs Feek, Violet Hubbard and Harry Brown.

Members of churches and chapels march together from Blofield School to the church, 1 January 2000.

he moved to Freethorpe School in 1956, Charlie took over that job. He gave it up in 2004. 'You shouldn't hold office more than six years but I was nearly 50 in the job!'

The Sunday school was run by Mr Futter, Mr Watson and then Harry Green from Brundall. Once a year Harry Green brought the silver band up to the chapel and gave an evening of music.

Then Mrs Flaxman took over and at one time had 40 children in the Sunday school. The children loved her. There were outings once a year to Yarmouth or Gorleston.

As kids we went to Sunday School in Blofield Heath in the morning, then the Mission Hall in the afternoon and chapel at night. I did that always till I was 17.

One of Charlie's Sunday-school teachers was Albert Nobbs. He took on the running of the little mission hall at Cuttons Corner and was the last in charge there before it closed down.

Roy Jermy's memories of the Cuttons Corner chapel

My sisters and I attended Chapel on Sunday mornings and one of our teachers in our Sunday school class was Miles Horner, who used to cycle from Strumpshaw, which was approximately three and a half miles each way. He was always cheerful and if we behaved ourselves he would give us each a sweet and we had a choice of aniseed balls or peppermint balls which he

kept loose in his pocket, very often they had gone sticky and were covered with fluff.

One of the reasons I attended Chapel was to have a lovely Sunday-school outing in the summer time and each year we returned to our same spot, which was at Gorleston on the end of the beach next to the long breakwater. They were very happy days!

Churches Working Together

In preparation for events and services at the millennium, representatives from Globe Lane Free Church, Blofield Heath Methodists and members of Blofield and Hemblington churches met regularly to talk and pray together.

A group still meets to pray for people in the villages and, specifically each month, for certain streets. Special prayers can be requested for those one feels are in particular need.

Brewster Court and West View sheltered housing and Manor Farm Home are all regularly visited, with services and home communion for those who wish. Members of churches and chapels help at Heathlands Day Centre. Blofield School pupils visit the church for Easter and Christmas services and the rector takes assemblies in both schools.

Each Palm Sunday a service is held in the afternoon, with congregations joining together from churches and chapels. Barry Raven, Alan Wakeman and Philip Unsworth take turns to host and arrange these services.

CHAPTER 4

Transport

Definition: 'A loke is an East Anglian term for a lane, sometimes a private one.'

Tom Whittaker, brother of Ivy Ryan, at one time lived in the thatched house on the corner of Church Road and Danesbower Lane. He worked for the county council surveying and mending roads.

Mr Norris 'Noddy' Waterson had a three-wheeled vehicle after the war, a 150–175 two-stroke Villier with a motorbike engine on the back and an open box affair at the front. He used it to carry grass and feed for his goats and rabbits.

Mr Merrison at Bay Bridge farm used a three-wheeled milk float.

Many people used bicycles to get to school and work and to carry loads.

Stanley Neve came round with milk churns on the

Cycles and a single car in the Street, 1936.

Emily and Alice Mincham, granddaughter and daughter of Godfrey Weston senr, in the lanes, 1924.

Road maintenance: Tom Whittaker (1898–1973) standing by a steam lorry, 1920.

handlebars of his bike and dipped out milk into customers' jugs, and 'Pudding' Moore cycled with a pail of food for his pigs hanging on the side of his handlebars.

Pattles at Cherry Tree Corner and Minters in Globe Lane ran taxi services.

Nearby is the railway: '1858; the Norwich to Yarmouth railway line station house has been erected at Brundall, 119½ miles from London.'

Little Traffic Then

Gerald Basey-Fisher remembers there was so little traffic that when his father used to approach the junction at the King's Head, coming from Brundall towards Blofield, he would just flash his lights and keep going.

Reported in March 1973:

55 houses are at present being built on six acres of land in Danesbower Lane, just off the main Norwich to Yarmouth road.

Until recently this land was filled with 400 apple and plum trees owned by Mr Percy Rope, a retired market gardener, who sold the land for housing. He recalls the days when Danesbower lane was no more than a cart track and the A47 was just a quiet road. 'As children we used to go on the main road and take down car numbers. If we got 12 all day we were lucky,' he said.

Blofield's Bypass

George (Did) Basey-Fisher recalled more recent traffic:

In summer there was a constant stream of holiday

Dove Cottage, 1981, which stood on the route of the bypass and was demolished.

The opening of the bypass bridge (shown below), October 1982. The schoolchildren had watched its construction.

Schoolchildren watch the cavalcade at the opening of the bypass in February 1983.

makers going to and from the Yarmouth area and all the large traffic. On Saturdays there was a tailback all the way from the Blofield traffic lights into Norwich.

Jimmy Dewing worried that the traffic along the Yarmouth Road would make it difficult for his wedding party to cross the road to get to the church on his wedding day. The patrol man on duty kindly held up the traffic to allow them to get to the church on time.

It was reported in 1983 that the bypass had been proposed before the Second World War.

Blofield born Ben Bussey was 16 in 1937 when he led horses for a team-man hoeing in Dunham's field. His job was to walk ahead and remove all the stakes marking the route of the proposed roadway.

At the same time, young Tony Rope was helping his grandfather to plant new plum trees in their orchard when he stumbled on a white-painted marker post in the undergrowth:

'Pull it out and chuck it in the hedge,' said grandfather Rope. 'There'll never be a bypass in my lifetime, nor perhaps in yours.'

View of the bypass.

(PHOTO BY MIKE PAGE, 2003)

CHAPTER 5

Streets and Buildings:
Where and How People Lived

Crossing the bridge at Witton Run one enters the parish of Blofield. Passing the crescent of houses built by Josiah Brewster for his retired farm workers and now forming the elegant frontage of the sheltered housing, we come to a row of varied villas built with views across the fields. Many of these retain the stable buildings once used for horses, ponies and traps.

The house now named Holly Bank is said to have originally been the toll-house, where money was collected from those using the turnpike road and at which a gate across the road would have ensured that all travellers stopped to pay the toll. The term turnpike is derived from the shape of the toll-bar, which resembled that of a pike staff.

Typical charges were a halfpenny for pedestrians, sixpence for horse-drawn carts and a farthing per head of cattle.

The village sign, 1968.

The old toll-house.

Witton Bridge. Cottages once stood here.

Brewster Court, 1964.

Drawing by Gordon Frosdick of South View.

The turnpike in 1936, narrower with high hedges.

Rose Villa, c.1900. Mr C.W. Bacon is holding the pony on which is sitting his son, the father of Eric Bacon (who later became Blofield School's headmaster).

Local cart traffic and journeys to church or to a funeral were exempt from toll.

Here, behind Mrs Harvey's house, the aptly named South View, was the bowling green for the King's Head public house. Mrs Harvey recalls that the main road has been widened several times:

The road had thick hedges on the north side and was narrower.

It was a busy road. The queues began in Thorpe. People thought they could overtake the hold ups and accidents often happened.

Rose Villa was once the home of Mr C.W. Bacon, of whom it was recorded in the October 1894 school log-book:

All the children were let out of school at 3.55 to partake of Mr C.W. Bacon's hospitality in the form of swings, shooting gallery, coker nuts and the other necessaries to a village fair.

He enjoyed opening his garden and entertaining the village children, and in 1896, when he had building

land for sale, he advertised the delights of dwelling in this 'salubrious' village. Who could resist such enthusiasm?

The Blofield Building Land

To the Editor
Sir, This splendid building site, approaching as it does near the highest land in Norfolk, and only distant about one mile from Brundall Railway Station, offering a rare opportunity for energetic builders and others, will shortly be brought under the hammer of that esteemed and energetic auctioneers, George Fitt and Co., Queen Street, Norwich.

For purity of air, salubrity of clime, and excellency of water, it cannot be surpassed, while the longevity of its inhabitants is something remarkable. It can be shown and proved that no less than 35 persons are now living whose united ages amount to 2,807, or over 80 years each.

The sale of this land in 65 building plots – over four acres in extent – with any amount of brick earth, will take place on Thursday next in a large marquee on the ground.

Free luncheon will be provided for all purchasers, with a free pass from Norwich and back; and as the property is so remarkably adapted for buildings that are so much needed, good bargains are inevitable.

> *Yours faithfully,*
Blofield   *C.W. Bacon*

Where the Globe stood there are now three houses, built following the inn's demolition in 1999.

For many years the Globe was a popular destination on a ride out from Norwich on a Sunday afternoon, being described in 1900 as 'a pleasure resort'.

It was plying business in 1776 and the following year a bowling green was opened. The new owner announced:

Robert Mayhem, from Norwich, begs leave to inform the Nobility, Gentry and the Public in general that he has entered upon that Pleasant House and premises known by the sign of the Globe, within six miles of Norwich , on the Turnpike road to Yarmouth... fresh stocks of best Port Wines... best endeavours... all Favours gratefully acknowledged – He has recently fitted up the Rooms, and has good beds for the Accommodation of Gentlemen on their travels.

In *Kelly's Directory* it was reported that, in 1845, mail arrived from Norwich every morning where 'the Post Office is at the Globe. Letters delivered and collected by the Great Yarmouth stage coach, horses being changed at Beighton White House.'

In 1850 the Acle, Martham and Norwich carriers passed through twice a week and the Norwich and Yarmouth Post Cart daily.

By 1854 letters arrived from Norwich at 8.00a.m.

The Globe, c.1880.

The Globe in 1960.

The Globe in 1910.

The court-house in 1936.

and were dispatched at 5p.m., and in 1890 there was a sub-Post Office run by Mr F. Rogers at Blofield Corner.

In 1845 Petty Sessions for the Blofield and Walsham hundreds were being held, with a visiting judge, alternately at the Globe and the King's Head each Monday. In 1865 the Swan was used; by 1890 the Globe was again the venue.

By this time a motor omnibus was passing through the village at regular intervals daily.

In later years a British Legion hut beside the Globe was used by the Scouts, who paraded from it to church services.

In 1905, when the law stated that court sessions might not be conducted within licensed premises, a court-house was built.

A children's party in the British Legion Hut after the war, c.1946. Those present include Len Layt, Roger Rope, Phyllis Cann, Gillian Rope, Marion Cann, Dorothy Bates, Brenda Layt, Vivienne Baynes, Joe Cullum, Janet Bates and Rex Hayton

With its cells, dock, judge's dais and waiting-rooms, the court-house was in regular use when the visiting judge toured the area. Ray Wales remembers, in 1957, bringing children under his care to the juvenile court, which was held monthly, and 'a grim place it was, although every effort was made to be less formal and the judge would meet the youngsters in his room at the back.'

Stocks Lane. *Miss Royal wrote in 1971:*

Bonfire Green. This grass plot at the south end of Stocks Lane is so called as in olden days a bonfire was lighted there to mark any great event.

Stocks Lane was so called because the ancient wooden stocks formerly stood at the top of the lane near the entrance to the main road – near a large and beautiful oak tree – long since taken down. The stocks were probably demolished about 1860. My mother as a young child could well remember an old occupant sitting in the stocks, and he was the last occupant as they were demolished soon after.

When Peter Eade, born in 1825, was growing up in the village, a parish constable was responsible for keeping law and order. 'To mete out punishment for minor misdemeanours Blofield had its own stocks, in a central and most public situation.' Sir Peter remembered seeing them occupied (for drunkenness, he believed) by an otherwise respected pillar of society:

And a very odd and striking sight it was to see this strong and powerfully built man sitting on the ground with his ankles locked in the stocks, and exposed to the pitying gaze of every passer-by.

The first licensee at the King's Head was Joseph Bane; great-great uncle to Miss Royal at Beech House.

Walnut Trees

Mrs Marion Jackson tells how her brother, Jimmy Knights, aged 14, had climbed a walnut tree in front of the King's Head to gather nuts for the publican when he fell, landing at her feet.

Three walnut trees outside the King's Head, 1915.

The King's Head in 1916.

Sid Brookfield used to park his fish and chip van (near where this van is seen in 1963). Muriel Read recalls running to buy 'tuppence and one', tuppence worth of fish and a pennyworth of chips.

The Swan, 1964.

Nut trees seem to have been a magnet to such nut collectors, with some tragic results – Albert Knights, aged 36, in 1933 fell from a walnut tree and broke his neck.

In the Plantations, past the school, there were hazel nuts to be gathered, and just visible from Lodge Farm was a walnut tree. It stood in the middle of a field and presented a challenge to boys to try to get walnuts without being spotted.

The Swan was rebuilt in about 1795:

21 May 1796. All that excellent new built inn... with a yard, stable and straw house belonging thereto.

Above, left and right: *The old Post Office, c.1905.*

Norman Marriot's cycle shop in the old Post Office buildings, c.1936.

An AA man at the crossroads, 1936.

These premises have recently been rebuilt at very considerable expense.

The licensees for its final 50 years until closure in 1982 were the Shred family, fondly remembered by Meg Morgan: 'Steve, Jessie and Brian have done more good in Blofield than a parley of parsons or a sortie of social workers all put together.'

In her kitchen Jessie cut hair for men and boys.

In his garden shed William Barrett also cut hair for the men and boys of the village (boys 4d., men 6d.), and mended their watches.

When the Globe ceased to receive deliveries of mail, alternative Post Office premises were opened opposite the King's Head. Mr Tuck ran the Post Office combined with a shop. When he moved into the present site in the Street, Mr and Mrs Charley Marriot took over in the old premises. Older residents can remember buying sweets from Mrs Marriot from Woodbine boxes on the counter. Norman, her son, mended bicycles in the buildings at the back in his spare time. After 30 years in the hands of the Marriots the shop was sold to Mr and Mrs Smithdale, who had it for 20 years.

Now a private house, the old Post Office retains the clock bought for the parish in 1916 after a series of disputes about its ownership. Mr Linford, the maker, restored and repaired it.

Arriving at the crossroads, we remember when pedestrians were assisted across this busy junction by the village policeman and an AA man stood on patrol at weekends directing traffic and saluting members with badges.

Turning into the Street at the King's Head corner, we follow the route taken by the main turnpike road. All traffic, including mail coaches, turned at the Griffin Inn on the corner of Doctors Road and continued along it on their way to Yarmouth.

It was only in 1810 that a new section of road was cut through the fields to connect up from the crossroads to the southern end of Doctors Road.

An elderly resident of the village, Miss Royal, explained in 1968:

Up to the year 1810 the Turnpike Road to Yarmouth went by way of the Street and Doctors Road, and out at Pattle's corner but in 1810 a straight road was cut through a cornfield and is now the main road.

The present butcher's shop [now houses on the corner of the Street and Doctors Road] *was then an old Inn, called the Griffin, and stage coaches stopped at the Inn on their way from Norwich to Yarmouth.*

The inn included the whole block of houses from the corner to the alley, and underneath the houses were the wine vaults.

Doctors Road, 1936.

Dr Kidd at the Grange in the 1880s.

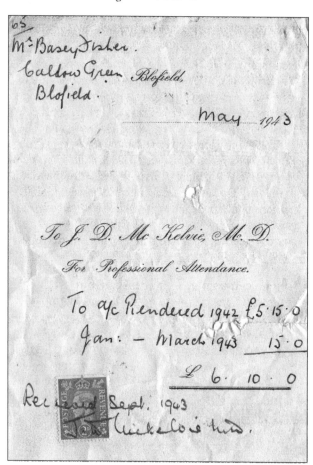

A receipt from Dr McKelvie, 1943.

Doctors Road

Village doctors have lived in Doctors Road for many years, two generations of McKelvies, Dr Evans and Dr Harris all having inhabited the Grange. Originally named the Shrubbery when Robert McKelvie lived there, the name was changed to the Grange during John Douglas McKelvie's tenure.

Dr Eade senr was surgeon in Blofield in 1863, Dr Kidd was surgeon to the Blofield Union workhouse at Lingwood in 1883 and George Torrance was listed in 1890 as Blofield's surgeon.

When Dr Evans moved from the Grange he built himself a bungalow with a separate, prefabricated surgery in the grounds. In a gale some years later, when one of the beech trees in the Manor House grounds fell onto it, the tennis club gained a pavilion from its remains and a new surgery was built.

When this surgery became too small a new building was erected in Woodbastwick Road in 1989 by Doctors Harris, Pilch and Miller.

At Cherry Tree corner, opposite Prospect House, was a cluster of cottages. Mrs Conlin:

I was born on Cherry Tree Corner. My dad was a cowman by trade but he used to mend shoes and clocks and watches across the road in a little hut on the end of Pattles's shop.

From 1929 Mr and Mrs Pattle ran the shop here, as well as a taxi business.

BLOFIELD DIRECTORY.		503
Bane Joseph, vict. King's Head	*Beer Houses.*	Hazel Samuel
Bane Mr Matthew	Brown John	Patterson Henry
Bayes John, thatcher	Gowen Benj.	*Joiners, &c.*
Barnes Fiddy, policeman	*Blacksmiths.*	Benns Thomas
Benstead Thomas, saddler, &c	Sawyer Richard	Broom John
Boast Robert, machine maker	Scurll Wm.	Lynes Joseph
Borton Rev John Drew, M.A.	Sizer Henry	Mingay John W
Rectory	Woodrow John	Rushmore Rt.
Brundell Wm. watchmaker	*Bricklayers.*	Stockings Wm.
Cheyne John, chimney sweeper	Clarke Wm.	(& builder)
Codling Wm. Hy. Union and magis-	Rushmore Anty.	*Plumbers, Gla-*
trates' clerk, supt. regr. & schoolr	Withers John	*ziers, & Painters.*
Coleman Timothy, vety. surgeon	*Butchers.*	Emms Hy. W.
Dobson Wm. hair dresser	Caston Wm.	Fisher Wm.
Eade Peter, surgeon and registrar	Hilling John	Fox George
Evans Thomas, cooper	Read Rt. jun.	*Shoemakers.*
Gapp Rd. Rant, schoolr. & tea dlr	Redgment Robt.	Bailey John
Garrard Misses || Jary Mrs gent		Bell Robert
Goulder Robert, *chief constable,* &c	FARMERS.	Bulley Robert
Greaves Rev Thos. Berkeley, vicar	Allen John	Clarke Charles
of South Lynn	Browne Wm.	Fox Richard
Haggata Leonard, vict. Swan	Browne W. jun	Gowen Benjamin
Lambert Thomas, tinner & brazier	Brooks Wm.	Harpley Tovel
Lincoln John, cattle dealer	Crow Robert	Shalders Robert
Lynes Jph. machine mkr. & wheelgt	Edrich Henry	
Mace Robt. gent||Parker Mrs My.	Ellis Henry	*Shopkeepers.*
Miles Lieut. Edmund, R.N.	Goulder Robert	Benns Thomas
Mingay John W. cabinet maker	Goulder Rt. jun.	BowenJas. baker
Overed John, farrier	(and maltster)	Bunn Samuel
Onslow Rev Wm. L.	Grimble James	Fisher Wm.
Postle Jeposaphat, relieving officer	Hardesty Wm.	Rushmore Robt.
Read Richard, cattle dealer	Lillystone Mrs	Salisbury Walter
Reeve James, schoolmaster	Long Robert	Tabor Edward
Ringer Mr John||Rix Mrs Bridget	Morris Wm.	*Tailors.*
Rising Edward, corn miller	Osborne Wm.	Crow Wm.
Rogers Mrs Sarah, corn miller	Postle Jsha. D.	Dunt Adam
Riches Thomas, hawker	Riches Thomas	Pyle Henry
Sillett Mrs Sarah, schoolmistress	Southgate Henry	Lusher Rebecca
Tuck John Hy. Esq. *High House*	Waters Robert	CARRIER.
Tuck Misses, gentlewomen		R. Waters, to
Tunmore John, sawyer	*Gardeners.*	Norwich, Sat.
Ward Joseph, vict. Globe Inn	Hazel Charles	

Entry in White's Directory, 1845. *Note the range of skills; sawyer, tinner and brazier, saddler and many more.*

Above and right: *Entries in Kelly's Directory of 1937 tell us who lived where and show the range of professions – butcher, tailor, cycle agent and wheelwright.*

A view of Cherry Tree Corner with Pattle's shop and Mitchell's tailor on the left, c.1930.

Mr and Mrs Fisher kept this shop from 1883, the Pattles taking over in 1929. Mrs Fisher wears a full-skirted gown and her husband a frock coat of light linen.

William Fisher was listed as a shopkeeper, painter and glazier in Blofield since 1850. By 1883 Francis H. Fisher was the draper and grocer.

Anny Stramik recalls:

As with the other village shops, dry goods like flour and sugar were kept in wooden drawers and scooped into sugar-paper bags for the customer. Out the back the bacon was stored in a meat safe, as there was no refrigeration, and it was brought in to a slicing machine. Biscuits, cigarettes and tobacco were all for sale and in a little room to the side, which is now a garage, pyrex

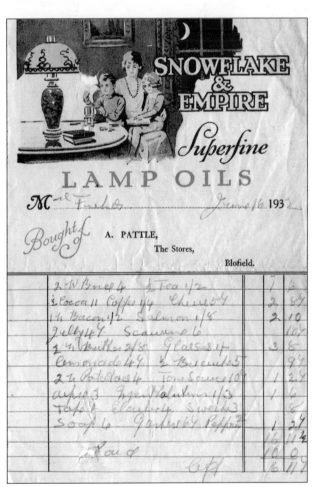

A receipt from Pattle's, 1932

kitchen ware, stockings, greetings cards and wool and cottons for mending were displayed.

Mrs Pattle was a tiny, frail-looking woman. Her mother came to stay when she was 80, living in the little house beside them, keeping a close eye on expenditure

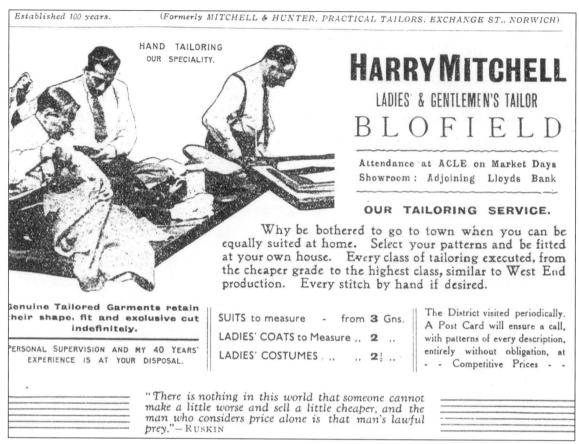

Established 100 years. (Formerly MITCHELL & HUNTER, PRACTICAL TAILORS, EXCHANGE ST., NORWICH)

HAND TAILORING
OUR SPECIALITY.

HARRY MITCHELL
LADIES' & GENTLEMEN'S TAILOR
BLOFIELD

Attendance at ACLE on Market Days
Showroom: Adjoining Lloyds Bank

OUR TAILORING SERVICE.

Why be bothered to go to town when you can be equally suited at home. Select your patterns and be fitted at your own house. Every class of tailoring executed, from the cheaper grade to the highest class, similar to West End production. Every stitch by hand if desired.

Genuine Tailored Garments retain their shape, fit and exclusive cut indefinitely.

PERSONAL SUPERVISION AND MY 40 YEARS' EXPERIENCE IS AT YOUR DISPOSAL.

SUITS to measure - from	**3** Gns.
LADIES' COATS to Measure ,,	**2** ,,
LADIES' COSTUMES ,, ,,	**2½** ,,

The District visited periodically. A Post Card will ensure a call, with patterns of every description, entirely without obligation, at - - Competitive Prices - -

"There is nothing in this world that someone cannot make a little worse and sell a little cheaper, and the man who considers price alone is that man's lawful prey."— RUSKIN

Advertisement for Harry Mitchell, tailor, 1936.

The turnpike (Yarmouth Road), c.1900. The white gate post is that of Lound Lodge (next to the Alley).

The Turret House.

and censoring any luxuries till she died at the age of 105. Mrs Pattle only outlived her by a few years.

Close by, Mr Mitchell plied his tailoring trade from the well-lit front room at Prospect House. The tailors sat cross legged on a raised work area, rather like a low table, to do their stitching.

Throughout the second half of the nineteenth century Blofield supported two tailors. From 1900 Harry Mitchell worked as a tailor, as did John Ferra and then Walter Read, near the school. Dressmakers used to work from home, two of them being Mrs Wilkinson at the Mill House and Mrs Massingham in

the Street, and a Spirella corset-maker lived and worked in a cottage near the school.

A succession of elegant villas along the Yarmouth Road brings us to an unusual property, the Turret House, which has an interesting story.

This fine house was built in 1831 by John Withers, a local bricklayer, as his family home and also, probably, to act as a show-piece of his building skills to those passing along the Turnpike Road.

Its design and construction were much admired by Sir Nikolaus Pevsner, the architectural historian. The house is unusual in that artisan families tended not to inhabit named houses until at least

Percy Rope's home, Danesbower House, in 1969.

This aerial view from 1964 shows Ellerbrook's Nurseries, the Edrich's Fox and Hounds Farm (at the top) and the Wakefield's house on the corner of Danesbower Lane and Lingwood Road.

The Fox and Hounds, late-nineteenth century.

the late-nineteenth century.

In the garden, the hollow known as the Dell was probably excavated to provide the bricks for Turret House and elsewhere.

When the family moved away the house was used for some years from 1888 as a ladies' school exclusively for the daughters of the local gentry and professional classes.

Pevsner also mentioned as being of architectural interest a fireplace bressumer (a breast beam supporting the wall above) dated 1732 at Owls Barn Farmhouse in Lingwood Road.

Along the road towards Lingwood, Percy Rope had extensive orchards and fruit fields and sold produce from his shop, a small room in his house.

The Fox and Hounds, which closed its doors in 1965, is remembered as a nice little pub with one bar in the room on the left. At the time of writing the owners of the property are David and Betty Pugh:

The original date of the building is unknown, but it is thought to have been built as a Public House as it is so similar to other hostelries owned by the long defunct Bullards Brewery.

The pub was called the Fox and Hounds. In August 1966 it was sold and converted to residential use and this was when the front, ground floor windows were changed to their present style.

The owners were the proprietors of the Old Beams

restaurant in Brundall and the property was renamed Crosswinds. A fire damaged part of the ground floor during this period.

In 1977 the premises were re-licensed as an Italian restaurant, La Locanda, owned and run by Antonio Masala and Bruno Puricelli.

We purchased the property in 1987, re-opening the premises as an English restaurant called Hobsons. 1994 saw us converting the property to its present use as a children's day nursery.

A house which stood by the entrance to Danesbower Lane belonged to Mr and Mrs Wakefield. On the 'pightle' of land they owned across the main road from the top of Fox Lane, the bullocks, driven out from Norwich on a Saturday, were left overnight to drink from the pond. Maybe the drovers visited the Fox and Hounds for their own refreshment! Next day extra helpers were needed, one of these being the young Dudley Edrich, who helped drive groups of 30 or so cattle to Myrus Sutton's farms in Upton, Halvergate and Panxworth, where they would be fattened up.

Jean Place remembers that:

Great Grandmother Broom kept the ale house called the Fox and Hounds. Her husband was coachman at Braydeston Hall. When he asked for a rise in his pay he was turned down but told that one of his children would have their school fees paid. This was about 1d. a week at that time. So Granny had her schooling paid for and she went on to an apprenticeship as a dressmaker. Later, when her husband died, she was able to support herself and five children by her dressmaking. At that time it cost 7d. to have a shirt made up.

One of those five children was Jean's mother, who was born in 1879: 'As a special treat she and her brothers and sisters were allowed to walk over from Strumpshaw to Blofield to go to the shop, with a bow fronted window, for sweets.'

Pony and trap in the Lingwood Road, 1913.

Right: *The bow-fronted window beside Honor House, 1940s. A line drawing of this, dated 1928, appears in the book* The Old Cottages and Farmhouses of Norfolk, *by Claude Messent, who designed the church lych-gate.*

Cottage in Lingwood Road, 1910.

After the war Mr Macdonald converted this room to a fish and chip shop, outside which folk would queue on a Saturday night.

George Mackerell remembers that at one time 'One-Armed Dick', the window cleaner, lived upstairs in the house with the bow window.

Blacksmiths

Older residents remember Sloddy Easter, whose blacksmith's shop was on the road to Lingwood.

Sloddy was a big man, always smartly dressed in a tail coat. The local boys used to creep up behind him and pull the 'tails'. He would shake his stick at the offenders, who enjoyed dodging out of reach.

Back in 1845 Blofield had four blacksmiths visiting various forges.

Michael and Greg Harvey, at Woodbastwick Forge, explain that:

A travelling smith would carry tools with him in a box or a leather bag. He would need tongs, a shoe-turning and a nailing hammer, a stamp and a pritchell, this was the long handled punch used to pierce the horse shoe. He would also need a buffer and pincers to remove the old shoes, nippers and a rasp and a measuring stick to determine the length of hot metal to be cut off. Probably he would carry a supply of nails and he would wear a leather apron to protect his legs.

As tractors replaced horses, so the number of farriers declined. Nowadays there are again a large number of horses in the country. Phyllis Jermy:

The blacksmith came round weekly or fortnightly when the Hemblington Hall farm horses wanted new shoes. They used to take them up there, tie them up and us children used to see it all steaming.

The mill along Lingwood Road, called Lubbock's Mill, was a smock mill with cloth sails. In 1833 John Woolterton Lubbock was the miller and was also a cabinet maker.

All that remains now is the Mill House where Jean Cann once lived. She remembers a very deep well.

The Mill House, Lingwood Road, 1950s.

Her husband George once went down to clean it out and remembers standing at the bottom on the wooden rim which had been used to construct the well and had been left in position.

Jean's mother used to put milk and meat in a pail half way down to keep it cool.

Church Road

Several large houses in Church Road stood in extensive gardens.

The rectory, built in 1806, is now known as the Old Hall.

Beech House is probably one of the oldest houses in Blofield and for a century or more from 1727 was the school, with its long front schoolroom, rather cold and damp.

When the house ceased to accommodate the school it was bought by the Royal family, the last to be resident there being Miss E.M. Royal.

During structural alterations made to the house during her occupancy a piece of ancient walling was uncovered which appeared to establish the existence of an earlier habitation on the site.

After her death in the 1970s an architectural historian at UEA visited and dated it to 1610 or 1620. It was probably once two houses and may have been timber framed. Its foundations may date as far back

The rectory, 1936.

Beech House in the early 1900s. For a century or more this was a school.

Above and right: *The Street, 1905.*

The Street, 1918.

The Street and Post Office, 1920s.

as the fourteenth or fifteenth century. Special 'scarfing joints' in roof beams date the roof to between 1625 and 1675.

Discoveries made when the house changed hands included marks still visible on the outer walls etched by schoolchildren in the early 1770s, and many old ink wells found in an old lavatory block in a corner of the quarter-acre garden.

Shops

In recent years the newsagent's shop has been run by Stewart and Sylvia Thompson followed by Steven and Sandra Mitchell.

Owners of the Post Office have been Mr Tuck, Mr Smith, Mr Hurd, Mr and Mrs Bates, Kenny and Heather Petley, David and Hazel Hadfield and, more recently, Paul and Dawn Tidy. At the time of writing it is run by Sheri and Rhea Singh.

Kahler's Shop
Mr Mackerell remembers:

There was a bakery at the back of the shop. Mr Kahler used to take the bread round in a cart. Harry Larwood, who lived down Frogs Hole, used to go up the city selling Evening Newses at the bottom of the Arcade. He was only about 5 feet tall.

He used to take the bread round the village in a basket and the basket was as big as he was. Before Kahlers had the shop it was Softleys and after them it was Hornagolds.

The Post Office in the 1930s.

The Swan and Kahler's shop, 1936.

Deliveries were done by Mr Wright and his son, Hokey. Mr Wright had a big Ford car and sold groceries and paraffin. Old Joe and Polly Gray both travelled by train from Yarmouth. She pushed her barrow round the village selling shrimps, cockles, winkles and herring and he carried a basket on each arm selling fish door to door. Mr Ferra delivered lamp and stove oil, selling it for 10d. a gallon.

The Kahlers, Hagues and Gedges lived on the south side of Garden Road. Opposite were Rope's orchards and a vegetable garden belonging to the Shreds at the Swan. Brian Shred was a marvellous gardener.

Olive Conlin remembers: 'It was an unmade road and we used to get really muddy going to school.' Mr Easter, a builder and carpenter who made all the coffins, lived right at the end of Garden Road, just into Globe Lane, where he had built two houses. 'My mum used to send me there for six penn'urth of turps and linseed oil because she used to have beeswax and make her own polish.'

Old Cottages Now Gone

Beside the bridge at Witton Run two cottages which stood by the road had a water pump. Further down a by-way, which was used by horses and carts, stood five cottages which used a well for their water supply. In one of these lived the Knights family.

When the loke no longer took traffic it became a footpath which one can still follow across the fields to Brundall.

Brenda Dawson explains that her aunt, Kitty Dossor (née Brown), lived in No. 1 Church Terrace in Church Road. Opposite her front gate was the entrance to the Granary. Before 1923, when Blofield had no Village Hall, this Granary was let to the rector, fitted out with stoves, lamps, curtains and used for the 'wholesome recreation our young people require'.

Mr Gowing was the farmer and landowner who 'did a public spirited thing when he bought the Granary and let it to the rector for the moderate rent of £12 per annum.'

Kahler's shop, c.1930.

View through cracked window of the interior of Kahler's shop, 1926. Leslie Hylton is on the left.

Left: *Leslie Hylton on his bread round, c.1927.*

Kahler's shop, 1910.

Garden Road in 1936.

View along Church Road, 1936. Church Terrace is on the right.

Mr and Mrs Knights and their grandson Henry at their cottage by Witton Run Bridge, 1930s.

Row of three cottages, c.1950, which stood beside where the Pinnacle House is in 2006.

Barbara Knights at the back of the houses in Globe Lane, 1967.

Outside her thatched cottage in Church Road, Mary Hogg and Connie Fisher, aged two, compare their art, September 1995.

The opening of the parish hall, 1923.

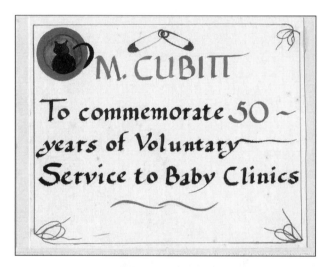

Miss Cubitt's years of service at the Infant Welfare Clinic.

Some older residents remember dances being held there and Arthur Pardon wrote in 2004, when he was 93, of boxing matches being staged at the Granary.

On the corner of Church Road and Danesbower Lane stand two thatched cottages which are all that remain of a cluster of old housing in this area.

George Mackerell recalls:

There were three cottages beside where Pinnacle House now stands, just into Danesbower Lane from Church Road. Here, at one time, lived Ted Vann, Mike Manthorpe and May Marjoram. These cottages ran back at right-angles to Danesbower Lane.

A Parish Hall

As a memorial to those who gave their lives in the First World War the parishioners purchased a field to be laid out as a recreation and sports ground. There was discussion about the need for a parish hall and Major and Mrs Harker stepped in and offered to build and equip one.

The Harkers employed Edward Boardman, the same architect who had carried out extensions to their home, and on the hall's completion in 1923 it was described as 'one of the finest village halls in the country.'

In 1929 a Red Cross Room was built beside the hall to house the Infant Welfare Clinics.

After Mrs Harker's death the hall became known as the Margaret Harker Hall.

Memories of the Village As It Was

In 1984 Mr Allen (born 1893) wrote:

Of course I remember a lot about the village; when there were two walnut trees in the Street opposite the present Post Office; all the old cottages which are gone – two harness makers' shops, three boot repairers, a watch repairer; when Canon Garrick lived at the Old Rectory with two maids, two gardeners and a coachman.

Mrs Sharman remembers:

On the corner opposite the King's Head was a piece of field and then a long stretch of corrugated iron surrounding a bowling green. It was later sold and three houses built there.

Maurice Gardener, who lived at The Dell, No. 2 Church Road recounted that:

The hall in 1936, renamed the Margaret Harker Hall.

Mrs Claxton in her house in the 1950s.

Church Road and the triangle of grass (heater piece) called Bonfire Green, 1936.

Edie Claxton with her mother and brother outside their house in the Street, 1950s.

Down the drive between our's and Roy Granger's house there was a shed which had been used by Mr Capp the cobbler. It had a fireplace where he melted the wax. When we began digging in the garden we were constantly digging up pieces of leather.

When Baden Hanton was 15 or 16, working on Mr Gowing's farm, he used to take one or two sheep in an old milk float, or a bullock in a truck, to Bickers's slaughterhouse off Doctors Road.

Roy Snelling remembers that when he and his mother cycled past, Mr Bickers the butcher always seemed to be standing outside his shop sharpening a knife.

When Mr Harry Edrich of Manor Farm died in 1943, after 22 years in occupation, the estate was sold. One of the estate houses was:

Lot 4
Brick and Tile Cottage
Situate in the Street, Blofield... containing: Living Room with Cupboards; Kitchen with Copper and Furnace, Stove, Oven and Furnace; Scullery and Two Sleeping rooms.

Outside – Two small Brick and Tile Store Sheds, Closet and Coal House;
as let to Mrs E.N. Claxton, at a rental of £15.12s. per annum, paid monthly.
The Sink in the Scullery is the property of the Tenant.

The Alley

Muriel Tallents remembers:

At the entrance to the Alley was a sloping cover to a cellar; children would sit on it and play at jumping off

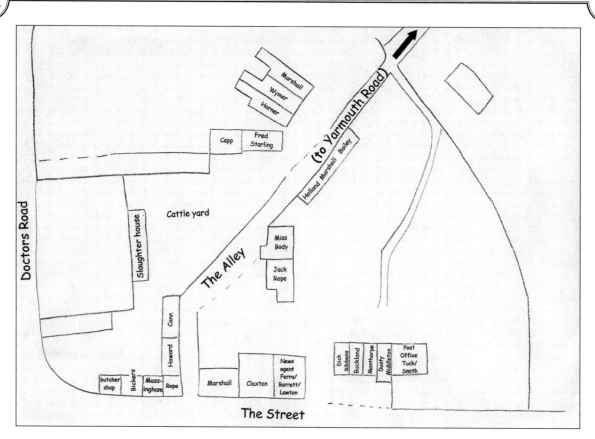

A map based on the 1845 Tithe Map but with the insertion of the three cottages furthest from the Street, which were built in the mid-1880s. Thanks to Muriel Tallents for supplying details for this map showing who lived there in the 1930s–50s.

Mr Bickers and staff at his butcher shop on the corner of the Street and Doctors Road, late 1920s. Behind were the cattle yard and slaughterhouse.

it. There were wells giving clear water. Miss Body, who lived in quite a large house, was a very kind soul who had been a missionary.

Vera Wardle (née Marshall): memories of 1943–49:

When mother and I moved into No. 3 Church Alley I helped her to do the weekly wash.

The well where we got our water was in the alley so our day began by getting hold of a handle each end of our tin bath and going to the well.

We would crank the old bucket up and tip the water into the bath, about four to five times, as much as we could carry back home, and it was tipped into the copper. The bed linen and so on were boiled and the copper emptied. Back to the well, repeat performance with the tin bath, back home and all the washing was rinsed.

Once more back to the well, repeat performance and a blue bag was added to the water and the linen soaked in that.

A big mangle stood outside with huge rollers and every item was put through the rollers as I turned the handle and pushed things through.

Then we hung it on the line, lovely and white, but oh, it was such hard work.

As there was no bathroom in those days we all bathed in that same tin bath putting it in front of the fire when the weather was cold.

Mrs Marshall with Violet and Eva, 1920s. There were two Marshall families in the Alley.

A house in the Alley, 1955.

Gordon Frosdick's drawing of the back of 'Altenau', seen from the Alley, 1997.

Braydeston Cottages

Baden Hanton worked for Mr Gowing of Braydeston Farm for 40 years.

He was born in No. 1 Braydeston Cottages and lived, when married, first at Waterlow and then in No. 5 Braydeston Cottages. Monica Law remembers:

Braydeston Cottages were initially for the workers at Braydeston Hall. A well provided clear water and washing was done using a copper in an outhouse. The cottages were sold off when the farm no longer needed them.

When the houses were built on Stocks Lane there were four houses on each side of the entrance to St Andrews Way and mustard fields where St Andrews Way was to be built.

Flax was also grown on that field during the war.

Chris Basey recalls his walk to school

In 1937, at the age of four, I started at Blofield School. The only way to get there from Brundall was to walk.

To be late was to run the risk of being caned, once you had left the Infants class, so if we were distracted and delayed by anything on the way we would arrive breathless from a mad dash down North Street to make sure that we got in line in the playground whilst the bell was still ringing.

We had to run the gauntlet of two lots of cows on the walk. First, Merrison's herd would be somewhere between Baybridge Farm and the entrance to meadows at the end of Highfield Avenue. It was difficult not to get our shoes covered in mud and cows' muck and not easy to get past them when they felt like using the whole width of road.

Once at Blofield, between Street Farm and the school, we had to negotiate Rope's cows. They always seemed to be the slowest cows on earth as they wandered along – usually on the pavement. Their route then took them past the school to the meadows behind the Plantations. If the school gate was open one of them was bound to end up in the playground to everyone's amusement.

Often our journey would coincide with Sergeant Harwood's departure from his bungalow on Blofield Road on his way for duty at the Police Station.

One afternoon on the way home we saw him struggling through the waist-high cornfield where the houses of Langham Green are now. He was trying to catch a man who we saw disappearing through the fence at the far side of the field. It was very exciting to be told later that he was an escaped German!

Of course we had to cross the 'turnpike' at the King's Head corner. Sometimes, a policeman would be on duty there and would see us safely over. At other times, mainly in the afternoons, the local AA Patrolman, Walter Westgate, would be there. His yellow motorbike and sidecar would be parked near to the signpost and he

Dennis (Tich) Buckland driving the cows from Street Farm down to Plantation Road in the early 1970s.

Braydeston Cottages, c.1970.

A policeman on duty at the King's Head crossroads, 1952.

The high bank across the road from the Post Office is visible beyond these buildings, 1940s.

Obadiah Smith outside Blofield Post Office, c.1940.

Mr Falgate worked in the Post Office.

would be on the alert to spot the cars with an AA badge on the radiator so that he could give the driver a salute. I was always glad to see him as, for some unknown reason, he would call me over and find a sweet for me in the depths of his uniform pocket.

Once past the King's Head we would walk along the pathway on top of a high bank as far as Garden Road from which we had a good view of Mr Smith sweeping the pavement outside the Post Office.

The paper shop was busy at that time of day and we

usually saw Mr Ferra loading his bike with papers for delivery. We could see inside where the newspapers and a few magazines were displayed on a counter that sloped away from whoever was serving behind it.

If we could hear the call of a jackdaw when passing The Swan we would be very wary. This was a tame bird which lived at the pub and had a reputation for swooping down to land on people's heads and for stealing anything shiny.

One very good reason for being on our best behaviour when walking through the Street was the possibility of being seen by one of the teachers, Mrs Turner, who would be on her way from Garden Road to the school.

Outside The Paddocks there was another high bank with a path along its top which also wound around a large tree beside the path. It was just about at this point on the journey that we might come upon Ben Bussey. This poor old man was a First World War veteran although we didn't know it at the time.

By the time we had reached the Reading Room it was possible to see the school playground and we would be horrified if there was a caravan parked there. This meant that the school dentist had taken up residence. He was a large man by the name of Wolfendale. He sported a large ginger moustache which, had we known, was a reminder of his distinguished service in the Royal Flying Corps. He lived at The Globe public house and, throughout the war, was a member of the Royal Observer Corps crew which manned the post on the old Brundall golf links.

He would be at school for a few days when every pupil would be called to the caravan in turn to have their teeth examined. It was scary enough to be sat in the enormous chair but any problem would receive very fast treatment – parents were not usually consulted.

If an extraction was thought to be necessary it was carried out there and then but, of course, not before an injection from (what at the time appeared to be) a syringe about twelve inches long!

The memories that I have of those winters are that there was a lot of snow which lasted a long time. There were long periods of very cold weather and the roads were like an ice rink as they received little treatment. None of the children in school wore long trousers so legs became chapped as well as hands and were extremely painful. Chilblains were also a problem. The school had no proper facilities for drying wet clothes and I well remember, in Mrs Rope's Infants' room, our coats and jackets hanging on the guard and the backs of chairs that were set in front of the large 'tortoise' stove that was the sole means of heat in the room.

Before reaching the school we passed the red brick cottages on the right where one of the front doors sported a decorative notice on which were the words 'Spirella Corsetiere'. We thought this a bit daring and it caused lots of amusement. Immediately past the thatched cottages, there was a wooden building, with large windows, at right angles to the road where Mr Read operated his tailor's business. Although he could not be seen from the road I knew that he would be sitting cross-legged on the big table sewing garments because he once made a suit for me. It's difficult to understand now why a growing boy should have had a tailor-made suit! I suppose it was for Sunday best. It was in blue pinstripe serge, fully lined, and I hated it.

There was one further distraction before going into the school playground and that was Mr Woodrow's blacksmith's shop, which was almost opposite the school gate. We would be attracted by the ringing sound of hammer on anvil and sometimes could watch showers of sparks when he pumped the bellows or removed something from the forge.

There was another interest just across his yard where, Mrs Woodrow would be preparing school dinners. She cooked our dinners in her kitchen and the older pupils helped her to bring them across to the school, where we ate them at our desks. I have memories of mince and cabbage. A favourite dessert was Manchester tart, which consisted of a pastry base lined with jam covered with a thick layer of custard topped off with brightly coloured 'hundreds and thousands'.

In an additional wooden classroom cookery classes for the girls were taken by a Miss Clarke, who lived at The Globe and, for the boys, woodwork was taken by Mr Crosby from Burlingham.

Ken Foulger remembers cattle walking from Street Farm twice a day, in mornings to a field down Plantation Road called the Lawn (anything but a lawn!) between two woods. One wood, cut down in the war, had chestnut trees and Ken would collect sweet chestnuts by the ton!

In the afternoons, after milking back at Street Farm, the cows went down North Street to a field at the bottom.

The Library

In North Street stands our village library, once a Wesleyan chapel which was purchased by the Baptists in about 1852. In the year of Queen Victoria's diamond jubilee the villagers were wondering how best to commemorate the event. Philip Steward, who then owned the disused chapel, offered to give it to be a Reading Room.

On 13 May 1897 the jubilee committee met:

It was announced, amid general applause, that P. Steward, Esq., had most generously expressed his intention of presenting the Old Baptist Chapel, at present his property, to the parish, to be used as a Public Reading Room and for other purposes which might be deemed useful. This munificent gift was enthusiastically accepted.

Jubilee Day, 22 June 1897

The day was ushered in by a merry peal on the bells from the old church tower. The children of both schools to the number of 265 assembled at the Blofield school about 9.30 and sat down to a substantial breakfast, to which they did ample justice. Joints of meat had been cooked and presented by many ladies and friends

Mr Read the tailor worked in the wooden building in front of the cottage. Mr Askham is selling ice-creams, c.1929.

The Reading Room, now our library, c.1930.

including Mrs Bellman, Bagshaw, Betts, Cassidy, Cooke, McKelvie, Pells, Steward and Rudd and also by Mr Weston…

After Breakfast the children, headed by the Rector, marched up to the old chapel, now being rapidly converted into the Reading Room. Here the Rector addressed the assemblage in a few words, and having received the key of the building, unlocked the door and declared the building open.

The children sang the National Anthem and, after three cheers for Mr Steward and the Rector, the very successful little celebration came to an end.

As a further treat for the school children Mr C.W. Bacon gave each child a newly minted penny.

At 2p.m. the Volunteer Company, under the command of Major Cooke, assembled at the cricket field and fired a feu de joie, a royal salute of 21 volleys. Thus, with three ringing cheers for our most Gracious Queen, our local celebration of the anniversary came to a close.

Library staff over the years, pictured together in 2006. Left to right: Sandra Dyble, Glynis McKay, Janet Smith, Ann Watts, Helen Gallaway, Jacqueline Ware, Margaret Harding, David Ivins, Julie Atkins.

The original intention of the Reading Room was 'to provide an opportunity for the young men of the parish to spend their winter evenings in reading and quiet social intercourse.'

Furniture being needed, gifts of plain Windsor chairs, tables and bookcases would all have been acceptable. Mrs Bellman of The White House gave 'a handsome table and a harmonium' – she was very generous with her gifts of harmoniums around the villages.

By October that year an annual subscription had been set at 4s., payable quarterly.

In May 1916, during the First World War, 'The Canteen' is described as follows:

A Refreshment and Recreation Room has been opened in the Reading Room, from 7–9 each evening Sundays included. The food is made in the parish and sold at cost price, the takings being about £1 a night.

By the 1920s older pupils at Blofield School were being taught skills such as carpentry, needlework, cookery and gardening. The girls' cookery classes were initially held in the Reading Room.

By 1942 it was used by the Boy Scouts, for Parish Council meetings and for practice by the Blofield Silver Band.

Every Wednesday afternoon it held the village library, books coming from the County Council Library. Miss Alice Foulger was in charge, with her son, Ken, helping to sort out the newly arrived books.

In June 1970: 'Congratulations to Miss E. Smith and her helpers for making Blofield Branch County Library so attractive. Numbers of borrowers are steadily rising.'

The library has gone from strength to strength.

The row of three cottages beside the old chapel were once one house, the chapel's manse, though a cellar below the middle cottage gave rise to the belief that it had originally been an ale house.

At one time Mrs Hilda Rope lived here, nearest to the library. She taught at the school and old pupils are very fond of her.

In the middle house lived Mr and Mrs Horner and, later, the Gowing family. Mr Fred Gowing remembered, when he first moved in, being told by Elijah Key, the owner of the properties, that as a young apprentice carpenter he had worked on a wooden extension at the back of the building.

Mrs Betty Basey (née Gowing) recalls Elijah Key coming up the back path with a pony and trap in which he would sometimes give the children a ride. He kept the pony in the meadow and barn, where the fish shop is in 2006.

Later, in the 1940s, Mr Bilby of South View owned the land behind the cottages. He used to drive down North Street very fast, his horse and cart almost out of control, and the children would rush to the fence to watch. The horse knew what it was doing and took him into the meadow by the barn.

Betty found it difficult to sleep on the evenings the silver band practised close by in the Reading Room!

Mrs Conlin lived in the white thatched house. She and her neighbours had to cross the road to fetch all their water from the well. 'It was pretty dangerous crossing the road because all the sugar beet lorries came straight through North Street.'

The red-brick house was home to Mr and Mrs Read. He was a tailor, well remembered by Mr Parker, who used to visit his grandparents in Blofield:

Mr Read's workshop stretched from the front of the house to the road. He made the lovely tweed suits for the local gentry and farmers and I can well recall seeing him cross legged on a big table sewing, while his

The thatched house with the well opposite, c.1909.

A heater piece at the crossroads, c.1910.

flatirons were heating on the open fire in the room.

The well stood on the pathway right opposite, on the other side of the road. The water was always so clear and cold. I was always fascinated to watch the handle of the drum whiz round as the bucket hurtled down to be stopped, just before it hit the water, by his hand on the winding drum.

In the 1930s, Peter Smith recalls, there was a centrifugal pump which you cranked to raise the water. Other villagers remember the hard work of fetching bucketfuls of well water. It was tempting to let the bucket hurtle down to the water, but then, when it hit the surface, it would come off its hook and there would be the lengthy job of retrieving the bucket and beginning all over again.

Most clusters of housing had a well they shared. The cool, sweet-tasting water is remembered, but also the hard work.

The triangular area of grass often seen at the centre of a junction was called a heater piece because the shape resembled the heater used when ironing clothes.

Continuing down North Street past the school brings us to a row of council-houses where once stood Rotten Row. A pretty thatched cottage is all that is left now of the older housing here.

George London had a sweet shop in a little hut and also mended shoes. He had suffered an injury to his leg in the war and had been sent on a training course by the government.

More old cottages on the opposite side housed Alice Foulger and her son Ken. Jimmy Woodrow, who kept chickens up behind the school, sold and mended bicycles from a wooden shop; Obadiah Smith bought his son Peter his first bike, a brand new Raleigh, the best in the catalogue, for £5.19s.6d.

Also living there was builder Walter Clark, who went round with a donkey and cart. When asked to take on a building job Walter would give the

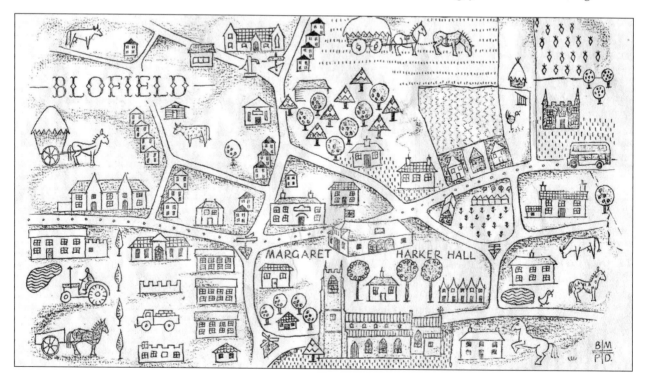

This 1951 map shows heater pieces at some road junctions. After the war prefabs were built in Shillito Road (not quite shown on this map).

Rotten Row and the view past the school down North Street, 1900s.

George London's little shop beyond Rotten Row, 1920s.

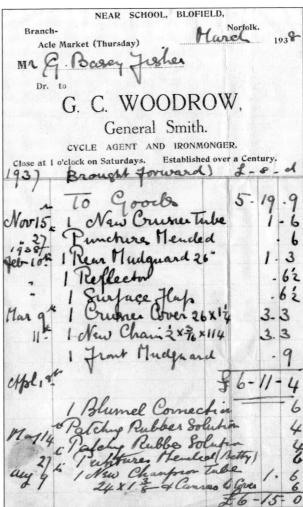

A bill from Woodrow's, 1938.

enigmatic reply: 'Me and my boy Billy will be round fore part of the week, about Friday.'

His son, Billy, conducted his saddlery business from the back of the Turret House, where the building abutts the loke.

Before the advent of the bypass North Street ran on towards Blofield Heath and was joined by Globe Lane to form Woodbastwick Road. At the point where it passed Callow Green it was at one time named Drove Lane.

The road passed Blofield House, home of the Chamberlin family, who ran the department store in Guildhall Hill in Norwich.

Robin Chamberlin was generous to Blofield Church in many practical ways, installing a heating system and setting up the choirboys' prize fund.

On the other side of the school, Plantation Road ran towards Blofield Heath, passing Blofield Lodge, once the home of the Morton farming family and venue for garden tennis parties.

Blofield Heath

The village sign was designed and painted by Gill Ward of the WI and made by Geoff Green and local blacksmith Michael Harvey on a base by Gerry Kelly.

George Woodrow's Forge, across Woodbastwick Road from the school, during demolition in 1973. Forge Cottage is being built behind.

Sidney Webb and his wife Madge (née Bickers) lived at Town Pit House, where their son Michael was born. Sidney's greenhouses covered the area where the Heath filling station now stands and a brick building was Sidney's potting shed. It was

Blofield House, home of the Chamberlins, c.1906. Mrs Chamberlin took this photograph and gave it as a postcard to her staff. A maid sent it to her mother explaining that it is Robin Chamberlin standing at the door. Eva Cornwell worked here in the 1930s and recalls a lawn mower pony then.

Heath Garage, mid-1970s. On the forecourt, Sidney is talking to his son-in-law, Leslie Riley.

Skaters on Town Pit, mid-1920s. Left to right: Harry Parker, Bob Newstead, Horace Webb, Wilfred Bulley.

Michael Harvey and Gill Ward with the village sign, 1999.

The Two Friends, c.1910.

early in 1960 that Sidney opened the garage. Behind Town Pit Mr Futter had a small market garden.

The Post Office was kept by Horace Webb. A series of postcard views were produced by him, as was a set by Mr Tuck, of Blofield Post Office.

Recent owners of the new Post Office have been Tracy and Paul Newman, followed by Michael and Gita Maher.

The Two Friends public house has been 'open since 1869, with a six-day beer licence only, until the closure of the Bird in Hand in 1930 when a full licence was granted.' Several extensions have been carried out, the licensees at the time of writing being Graham and Tracy Hobden.

Mill Road

The deanery magazine for March 1914 advertised the

Youngman's shop and old Post Office beside the Two Friends, c.1910.

View along Mill Road, with Mrs Bailey's house and shop (on the left) and the Rogers' house (on the right), 1920s.

subjects for the Debating Society's next meeting and posed the question:

Is it true, by the way, that all the intelligence of Blofield resides in the neighbourhood of Mill Road? We have heard it said so in the Society and there have not been enough members from the other hand to dispute the proposition effectively!

Mill Road contained a number of attractive old properties with large gardens, well spaced out, with many orchards and pastures. In years gone by everyone grew their own vegetables and fruit. 'We didn't need a greengrocer's shop, we grew everything. Mother might have a tin of salmon and a tin of peaches but everything else was fresh.'

The orchards and pastures have vanished as lokes and closes of newer housing have appeared.

Mrs Bailey's shop is remembered by many people who, as children, went in for sweets. It was run by Mrs Bailey, whose daughter Dolly was the infant teacher at the school.

Phyllis Jermy recalls: 'A bell rang when you went in there. If I had a penny to spend I used to get quite a lot because things were only a farthing then.'

In 1966 **Mr and Mrs Neave**, owners of a smallholding in Dyes Road, bought what had been Mrs Bailey's house and little sweet shop from which to sell their vegetables and produce. For two years they used these premises as a small shop with storage space upstairs.

After rebuilding the property they opened their supermarket-style village shop in 1969.

The **Rogers family** were millers in Mill Road for about 100 years. In 1850 Sarah Rogers was listed as miller, followed in 1864 by Francis and in 1883 by William. In 1900 and 1908 William was running the mill by wind and steam. Ernest Rogers took it over in the 1920s and '30s.

One resident of Mill Road, **Mr Martin**, suffered from TB and lived the outdoor life in a type of summerhouse to benefit from fresh air – thought to

Bulley's Cottage, c.1903, now Villavon Way. Robert John Bulley can be seen, along with son Herbert and wife Sarah.

Neave's shop in Mill Road, 1969.

be the best treatment. Revolving shelters, available at the time for anyone not eligible for sanatorium treatment, could be turned so that the open side faced away from the wind.

In **Blofield Corner Road**, Holly Lodge was once a dame-school where the daughter of the house taught local children, who payed 1d. a week when it could be afforded.

A plantation of trees stretched along the southern

A tower mill stood just off Mill Road, 1924.

Blofield Hall, 1905.

The Bird in Hand, c.1875.

The Trowel and Hammer in Blofield Corner Road, c.1910.

edge of the road. When this was removed Mr Waterson built his own house (named The Style) using some of the timber. His was the first house to be built along that side of the road. He used his three-wheeled vehicle to cart water from Town Pit for the building work.

Market gardens stretched along most of the northern side of the road.

The Trowel and Hammer public house, which closed in 1930, stood on the road to Little Plumstead.

The story is told that, because it was in a low-lying position where water gathered, the bar used to flood. Water would come up between the pamments (large tiles) on the floor, unfortunately bringing with it a reek of stale beer.

It closed as a public house in about 1930 and became three separate homes. Janet Frankland lived in one until she was 18, next door was the Shingles family and nearest to the road were the Kiplings.

The laundry in Laundry Lane, initially a private laundry for Major Harker's household at Blofield Hall, became public from 1936. Mrs Freeman ran it, her husband George being a tailor.

Later, Roy Snelling converted it into the small beginnings of what was to become his extensive radio and TV business.

The Bird in Hand, a public house from 1836 until 1930, had its own bowling green at the back. In 1915 the licensee was Joseph Colk, and in 1927 Herbert Wright was fined £2.0s.6d. for selling out of hours.

It is said that when cattle were driven along Mill Road to the marshes, the men stopped here to refresh themselves.

A thatched cottage at **Cuttons Corner** was home to Mr Cutton and later the Barber family. Mr Cutton's son built himself a house next door and gave land in front of it for the erection of the chapel.

In the garden of his parents' old, thatched, wattle and daub cottage Arthur Barber built the house where he and his wife Sylvia live at the time of writing. Sadly the old house was condemned and knocked down.

The Bird in Hand, c.1928. Left to right, back row: ?, ?, ?, Mr 'One-Eye' Townsend, ?, 'Hokey' Wright, ?, ?, Herbert Bates; middle row: Mr Barber, Mr Barber senr, ?, Sam Mayer, ? Jermy, ?, ?, Mrs Wright, ?, ?, ?, ?, Tom Whittaker, ?, ?; front, seated: ?, Peggy Wright, Audrey Wright, ?, ?, ?; on ground: ?.

Mr Cutton lived in this thatched cottage. and then the Barber family. Photograph, 1962.

Hemblington Hall and farm, 1964.

Hemblington and Pedham

The Domesday recording of Hemblington reads:

In Hemblington 2 freemen at 60 acres of land. Ralph the Constable [held them] before 1066 with the full jurisdiction, but Bishop A[e]lmer had the patronage only of 1. Now Bishop W[illiam] holds 1 and earl R[alph held] the other. Value 2s.

Hemblington Hall bears the initials of William Heath and is presumed to be the eighteenth-century seat of that family. Old estate maps show gated roads at

entrances to the parkland which stretched in front of the hall, with an avenue of trees leading towards the church. The 1845 Tithe Map marks formal gardens.

Mr Youngs bought the Hall and farm in 1919. In the 1920s and 1930s Youngs and Westons were the principal landowners in Hemblington.

How the council-houses in Hall Road came to be built in the 1930s

When Mr Youngs needed to house his workers he spoke to Mr Whittaker, a council man who lived in Hemblington Hall Road, who suggested that Mr Youngs sell the council a piece of land on which they

Mr Youngs of Hemblington Hall had just bought this lorry from Delves in 1934. Jimmy 'Brassy' Brown is the driver.

Mr and Mrs Youngs and their four daughters, 1913. Left to right, standing: Daisy, Beulah, Mrs Mary Youngs, Margery; seated: Alfred John with Ella.

Pedham, 1924.

Pedham Dam and Keeper's Cottage, c.1920.

The bridge at the end of Cinder Muck Lane, possibly 1890.

would build five houses.

Arthur Jermy's family was one of the first to move into one of the four-bedroomed houses. There were 13 of them – parents and 11 children – and he couldn't quite imagine how they had all managed in a cottage at Wood Farm!

Eric Bates's grandparents lived in Hemblington

The gamekeeper's hut, 1912. Jack Cutler, aged 13, is on the left.

Hill and Eric used to cycle to Clamps butcher shop in South Walsham and return along the byroads, opening and closing three sets of gates, calling to see both sets of grandparents.

Pedham is described in a directory in 1845
A scattered hamlet which derives its name from a fine lake or dam, that covers ten acres, and has a beautiful waterfall, ornamented with grottoes, arches, piles of stones and clumps of trees arranged in the most fantastic manner

Here is a school at which Mr Wright a Royal Artillery pensioner teaches 30 free scholars for £5 a year paid by the incumbent.

The other residents are Edward Bayes, joiner; Wm Gedge, bricklayer; and Rt Thurtle, gamekeeper; and those at Hemblington are Thomas Coleman veterinary surgeon; Jeremiah Cutton, shoemaker; Charles Gillett Rope, farmer; James Smith, wheelwright; and Nathaniel Weston, farmer.

Bryant's 1826 map shows 'Pidham Mill'. Graham Martin explains that Peatty Mill, later Pedham Dam, was the site of a watermill. Around the late 1800s a fashionable grotto was created using the water which had previously turned the mill wheel.

The watermill had served a number of villages, one of which, in the Domesday Book, was called Leather. This is now named Blofield Heath.

Graham recalls go-karting down Sally Bush Hill, and others remember childhood picnics and happy days spent playing by the bridge at the end of Cinder Muck Lane. Youngsters, alone or with their mothers, took jam sandwiches, played, and found trees to climb. Water poured in a waterfall from a lion's mouth and the children used to dam the stream for swimming.

Terry Starking's uncle, Jack Cutler, who lived there, had a lot of remedies, and would say to Dr Gray, 'You know how to treat that Doctor? Put a little treacle on it.'

The people of Pedham

Roy Jermy shares his memories of those living in Pedham as he grew up there in the 1930s and 40s:

Billy Bugden was a length man on the roads and in later years he worked for May Gurney driving a steam dredger on the broads.

He used to go ferreting in the fields carrying a large special spade to dig the rabbits from their burrows. He kept three or four hives of bees, making his own hives and round skeps from wheat straw and also constructing the frames for the bees to make their honeycombs on. I used to help him when the time came round to take the honey from the hives.

Billy's daughter, Vera, recalls that she was sent one day to Langley's toy shop in Norwich for a stencilling set so that her father could make a sign for his front gate. This featured in the local press and in later years appeared in Woodbastwick.

Waldo White and George Moor, who was known locally as Puddun, were both road men. In Puddun's spare time he kept geese on a meadow along the side of Cinder Muck Lane by a large stream which led from the waterfall. Here we used to paddle and have our picnics. We were very frightened of the old gander which used to chase anybody.

Many people had nicknames. Mr Evans, a thatcher by trade, was known as 'Brotch' or 'Stiffen'.

A keen gardener, Mr Clisp always wore a green baize gardener's apron.

Robert Dunch worked in Norwich as a Corporation gardener. He looked after the Castle mound gardens, mowing them with a scythe after the daffodils had finished flowering.

Robert's son, Edwin, points out that Robert wore football boots so as to get a grip on the sloping grass.

Bob had a horse and trolley which he used twice a

BE YE GORN
OR BE YE CUMIN
BE YE ARLY
OR BE YE LERT
DORNT FUGIT TU
SHUT THIS GERT

A sign on Mr Bugden's gate, 1970.

week to take produce to the shops from his market garden. Dick was a reliable horse, and when a stranger to the district once needed to travel back to Blofield but did not know the route he was told, 'Just sit up there and leave it to Dick.' He was safely delivered.

One year Edwin and Roy Jermy used the trolley to collect a Christmas tree given to the school by the Pedham estate.

Roy continues:

Mr Eric Martin lived with his sister, Edie. He sold almost everything in the grocery line, including paraffin and creosote, which he kept in a shed outside his shop. The only trouble was that he never had a sink to wash his hands after serving various items. You had to be careful when to order, as you could taste either paraffin or creosote. He also had a trade bike on which he would deliver various groceries, including cans of paraffin hanging from the handlebars.

Mary Oliver recalls that Eric Martin sold a limited range of groceries, threads, odd bits and bobs:

Maybe he had been gassed. In some way he was a casualty of the First World War. His sister lived with him and appeared to be looking after him.

He used to go round the village with a trade bicycle with a big box on the front with a selection of things he thought the elderly and housebound might want to buy.

And Brenda Dawson comments: 'Mr Martin hired a Red Car coach and organised outings on a Sunday to Luton Ho, Britannia Pier, to the theatre and many other places.'

More of Roy's memories:

We used to watch Billy Cockrose chopping sticks for his fire so quickly we thought it was a wonder he had any fingers left on his hand. Hanging from a large hook on his wall was a stirrup pump, called our fire point, which was to be used if incendiary bombs were dropped into the village.

Eric Mayer lived in Rose Villa, which had a large open-topped chimney, leading from his lounge fire. In the wintertime, when the snow was on the ground, we used to make large snowballs and throw them into the top of the chimney and the snowball would fall straight into the fire. Once we had thrown them we never stopped running.

Bert Wright was one of our village postmen. Mother told us that his house used to be the village shop.

Louis Hylton lived in a farm worker's tied cottage, No. 142. It was one of only two cottages in the village with a number. The other, No. 167, was along Hall Road, Hemblington. Standing a mile and a half apart, they both belonged to the estate and followed its particular numbering system.

Mr Hylton was a very hard-working man, both at

Louis Hylton outside No. 142 with five of his eight children, 1925.

Billy Bugden on the trolley at the Willows in Pedham, 1938. Left to right: Emily Dunch, Beaty Day, Donald Day, Dick (the horse), Bob Dunch and Billy Bugden.

work and also in his spare time. He used to mend boots and shoes, not only for his family but also for most of the village people. Most evenings you would hear him hammering the hobnails into heavy boots. He would cycle to Norwich to get the leather and hobnails on Saturdays and bring them home on the handlebars of his bike. He was known as the village 'snob' (boot and shoe repairer). He also mended bicycles and repaired punctures and he was the village chimney sweep. He lost two sons during the war, Cyril and Ronnie. Bob was also a prisoner of war for over 3 years.

The toilet was at the bottom of his garden and was a double one with two seats side by side, one with a large diameter and one with a small, and the wooden bench seat would be scrubbed until it was almost white.

The Hyltons had a large apple tree in their garden and the apples were known as 'Green Roland'; it was a good eating and cooking apple. The tree is still in the garden today and still bears lots of fruit.

Albert Woodhouse, a farm labourer, worked for Godfrey Weston at Gables Farm.

Mr Jimmy Feek was a carpenter and undertaker. He made coffins in the workshop at the top of his garden. Mother used to say 'Somebody has died as Jimmy has just gone past with his measuring stick.' We also knew of a death as the Hemblington Church bell was tolled. Tradition in the village was that on the day of the funeral all the cottages would have the blinds or curtains drawn across the windows which faced onto the road. Also, when the hearse passed through the village, if we were in the road, we would stand still and remove our caps in respect.

Jimmy's daughter, Letitia, lived outdoors in a hut as she suffered from TB.

Bert Youngman, who kept Little Plumstead Post Office, cycled to church and, on Armistice Sunday, sounded the Last Post during the service.

Gilbert Hambling was a scaffolder by trade, which was a very skilled job as the poles were wooden and they all had to be secured correctly by rope.

A painter and decorator, Russell Mayer, worked for many years at Little Plumstead Hospital.

Archie Poll, a gardener, worked for Major Harker at Blofield Hall.

Mrs Marshall kept the shop on sand-hole hill.

Reggie Newstead was a postman by trade and after delivering mail in the local area for several years, he then got promotion and used to travel up to London on the night train to sort the mail as he was travelling back to Norwich.

Reggie and his wife Peggy were ballroom dancers and they used to teach in our local dance hall. He also taught the ATC cadets how to tap out Morse code and use the Aldiss lamp for Morse code.

Mr Herbert Norton worked for Ernie Morse, who was a well-known rose grower in Brundall. He was a very good, conscientious Chapel preacher at our local Chapel. He would never do any unnecessary work on Sundays and he would always be up early Sunday mornings to cycle to the Chapel to light the tortoise stove to get the Chapel warm for the service. He would then cycle home, have his breakfast, and then return around half past ten to start the service.

His daughter also played the Chapel organ with another lady by the name of Rosie Merrison who lived at Cuttons Corner.

Life in Pedham

When we moved into our cottage Molly's father made a 'safe', as we had no refrigerator in those days, for keeping meat, milk and butter in. It was fixed on the north side of the wall outside and I cannot remember any food going off. It was made from wood and the sides and front were made with galvanised perforated zinc for keeping flies and insects out.

We did not have mains water supply but we had a pump outside our kitchen door where the water was

George, the local policeman, and Joan Bailey in the early 1900s.

lovely and fresh and drawn from a deep well.

In the 12 council-houses there was no mains drainage or septic tanks. All night soil, as it was called, had to be buried in the garden and all the dirty water and washing water had to be emptied into a large muck hole. When it was full it was covered over and another hole had to be dug. There was one well in the centre of the houses to supply all the water needed to bath and wash, as well as drinking water for 24 adults and 28 children.

Our rent at the time was 7s.6d. per week, which in today's money would have been about 37p.

How the parishes have grown
Population figures

	Blofield	Hemblington
1931	1,171	36
1951	1,292	224
1961	1,479	211
1971	2,285	250
1981	2,635	262
1991	3,276	305
2001	3,221	316
2004	mid-term estimate	
	3,305	320

CHAPTER 6

Wartime

Threatened by invasion around its coast, this part of Norfolk has, through many European conflicts and wars, been prepared to defend itself.

Military badges and buttons have been found that point to the existence of a Blofield Yeomanry in 1790.

Mr George Mower, headmaster at Blofield School, was very patriotic and closely followed all national crises, keeping his pupils informed.

During the 1899 Transvaal crisis: 'In Blofield school the children were encouraged to contribute pennies and halfpennies to the Transvaal War Funds.'

In 1900:

... girls knitted balaclava helmets for use of the volunteer company going to the front in South Africa. The

James Gowing (1865–1919) at a military camp, probably at Gorleston, in the late 1800s. The uniform is believed to be that of the Norfolk Yeomanry.

wool was bought with money collected by the girls, while the boys helped by adding stamped envelopes.

On Tuesday the surrender of Cromje and 4,000 Boers and on Thursday the Relief of Ladysmith. The scholars sang God Save the Queen.

In May 1900:

On Thursday morning the scholars assembled at the usual hour, but the Master having received a telegram notifying that Mafeking had been relieved, and seeing also that it was the Queen's birthday, the school was not opened. All went into the playground, where the National Anthem was sung, three cheers given for the Queen and the children were dismissed, to carry the good news home.

Parish Life during the First World War

From the 1916 school log-book:

Truancy. Frederick Dewing, Russell Manthorpe and Percy Long were absent from school (truanting) on Tuesday, staying away to see Royal Scottish Engineers come into the village.

Mr Fred Allen wrote down some of his memories in 1984, when he was 91. He had lived in Blofield for the past 89 years and at that time lived in St Andrew's Close.

He remembered when 'the volunteers in their red tunics used to drill on the meadow which is now Garden Road.'

During the First World War, when he was sent home with an injured ankle, he attended a hospital in Brundall every morning for treatment before he returned to the field of action. The war hospital he attended was in Brundall House (later demolished for the Finch Way estate), which operated as a Voluntary Aid Department auxiliary hospital from October 1914 to October 1916. It had been placed at the disposal of the Red Cross Commandant, Mrs Margaret Harker of Blofield, by its owner, Mr ffiske. The hospital had 40–50 beds and, during the time it was open, admitted 712 patients for convalescence.

Sad accounts of injuries and death in the school log-book, October 1916:

The Master has to report the deaths of George Burdett

Members of the play Patriotic Pence, *1918.* First on left, back row: *Kathleen Hague, later Turner;* first on left, middle row: *Miss Foulger;* front row, at extreme right: *Dolly Dale, later Minter. Note Flora House in the background, home of the Spantons, threshing contractors.*

and Reginald Gunns who both died from wounds received in Flanders. The former, who had been in hospital in London, was brought home and had a semi-military funeral; while Reginald was interred in France. Both lads were old scholars, had been in business, and were highly respected.

And a comment on our vulnerability in Norfolk, from the July 1916 deanery magazine;

Special thoughts for those who protect the east coast from invasion.

We on the East Coast have a lively perception of what we owe those who have fought for us in the North Sea.

From the school log-book, March 1917:

Miss Mower and Miss Foulger have organised a series of relays whereby half a dozen girls in turn bring comforts – eggs, cakes, buns etc – on Friday mornings these comforts being forwarded to Ward 10, Thorpe Military Hospital, for the soldier patients. The children are very enthusiastic in the cause.

Some of the girls are preparing songs, dances, recitations etc with a view of entertaining the patients of Ward 10 on the Wednesday afternoon of Easter week.

Hester Larke, in the school holidays of 1917 and 1918, used to take churns of milk into St Andrew's Army Hospital in Thorpe, going in the mornings at 7.30. She used a milk cart belonging to the Gowings of Braydeston Hall and Church Farm, who also had land at Hellesdon.

Hester Larke in the milk cart, 1918.

In October 1917:

During the week the scholars have brought 5cwt of horse chestnuts to school which have been forwarded to Norwich in accordance with instructions from Minister of Munitions. It has been asserted that one ton of chestnuts will save half a ton of grain for human consumption [by feeding them to the horses].

In 1917 Mrs Griffith of the Manor House offered prizes to the older schoolchildren for the best essays on 'How I can help to win the war', and in 1918 she produced a children's play, *Patriotic Pence*, raising money to provide a tablet for those of the parish fallen in the war.

Since 1915 she had worked for the Patriotic Kitchen Garden Association, which aimed to prevent wastage of food in households, to increase food supply by vegetable growing, poultry farming, jam making or fruit bottling and to distribute to the needy and the hospitals.

When working parties were set up in 1916 preparing parcels and letters to send to all Blofield men at the front, long knitted scarves, helmets, mittens and socks, cigarettes, chocolate and soap were sent, and 'Mrs Griffiths has sent a little writing case with paper, envelopes, and a small almanack to each man. Miss Richmond sent lavender bags to bring memories of home.'

The subject of insufficient manpower on the farms was touched on in the August 1918 edition of the deanery magazine: 'Harvest help from schoolboys. Fifty schoolboys aged 15–16 are spending August at Blofield Lodge to assist in the harvest work in the locality.'

Chris Basey writes about the two world wars in Blofield and Hemblington:

Remembrance

As early as August 1915 the Blofield Deanery Magazine stated:

A beautiful oak frame, intended to take the photographs of Blofield men who are serving in Army and Navy, has been hung in the Church porch. The photographs are

The wooden war shrine, dedicated in August 1918, was moved inside the church when the stone cross was erected.

coming in steadily and will form a most interesting collection. When the war is over we hope to photograph the group and to preserve the picture and the names as long as possible.

In July 1916 it was reported in the magazine:

Our second photograph frame is nearly full already and if every one of the men who have gone from this parish to defend us, were represented here we should require still more room.

Sadly, that valuable collection of photographs has not survived. By June 1918 it was proposed:

... to erect a War Shrine in some part of the parish to keep the memory green of those who have given their lives in the war, until such time as a permanent memorial can be raised in the parish.

The shrine was, in fact, erected outside the church on the site of the present war memorial. It has been preserved and is now inside the church.

After the war, in May 1920, plans were drawn up for the War Memorial:

The Cross of silver granite from Cornwall has been executed by Mr Potter of Norwich and will be unveiled on Sunday May 16th. The Dean of Norwich (Dr Willink) has promised to preach at morning service on 16 May and it is hoped that he will dedicate and unveil the Memorial Cross.

Names from our parishes on the Blofield War Memorial
1914–19

Philip Barber	Ernest Ling
Reginald Blyth	Ernest Lynes
William Brown	Charles Marler
George Burdett	Benjamin Marshall
Alec East	Benjamin Newstead
Thomas Farman	Bertie Newstead
Walter Foulger	Robert Payne
Harry Gostling	Nelson Rose
William Gowen	James Shreeve
William Green	Alfred Simmons
Reginald Gunns	Arthur Smith
Percy Hall	Frederick Symonds
William Hanton	Russell Symonds
Herbert Houghton	William Turner
James Jaggs	Arthur Ward
Bernard Limpus	Herbert Waterton

The Dedication of the War Memorial

From the deanery magazine, 16 May 1920

A memorial in honour of the 32 men who lost their lives in the war was unveiled and dedicated at the north west angle of the church on the spot formerly occupied by the

The dedication of the war memorial, 16 May 1920.

war shrine, now moved just inside the main entrance to the church.

The ceremony commenced with a service inside the church where accommodation could not be found for all comers. Seats had been reserved for relatives of the fallen, for ex-servicemen, Boy Scouts and Girl Guides. A shortened form of evensong was conducted by the rector the Rev Arthur Shillito, the lessons being read by Rev T.C. Spurgin of Strumpshaw and the Rev T.H. Carson of Little Plumstead. The Dean of Norwich gave the address and the Rev C.M. Chamberlin of Brundall was also present.

To the singing of the hymn 'Let saints on earth in concert sing' the choir, Girl Guides and Scouts moved out of the church to the memorial A large gathering had already assembled. The cross, which was covered with the Union Jack, was unveiled by Major Harker, at which the Guides, Scouts and ex-servicemen saluted. The Dean then dedicated the cross 'To the glory of God and in grateful memory of the men of this parish who gave their lives in the Great War.'

The 'Last Post' and 'Reveille' were sounded by Mr Ernest Gedge.

Wreaths and bunches of flowers were then brought forward and laid at the base of the cross by relatives, friends and sympathisers. During the singing of a hymn, the concluding prayers and Benediction by the Dean, the Union Jack was displayed at half-mast on the church tower.

Our Parishes in the Second World War

Collections were made to support the families of minesweepers. Fishermen, already with dangerous jobs, found their trawlers commandeered for

---

BLOFIELD POST OFFICE,

August, 1941.

If the Invader comes, 'Stay Put'

To the Occupier,

In the event of the above emergency arising, you will no doubt do as requested and "Stay Put." All the same you will be wondering what is to happen about "Food."

On this point you may be satisfied that there are emergency stocks in this village sufficient for all and a scheme in hand to distribute same fairly.

Briefly this is what will happen.

On being warned of an emergency by Wardens or Home Guard. You will proceed to place stated overleaf, taking your Ration Books. You will then be issued with Emergency Rations. Take care of this issue, it constitutes your last line of defence to be eaten last of all. The able bodied will no doubt help the aged and fetch their Rations.

Shops will be closed to allow stocks to be requisitioned and proportioned. A notice as to time of re-opening will be posted on shops concerned. You will then get your share of ordinary Rations from shops and places stated overleaf.

We have no Baker in the Village so make arrangements to bake bread in some form.

May I ask for your co-operation in this scheme without which only chaos will result.

Also I shall be pleased to answer any enquiry in the meantime.

O. E. SMITH,

Voluntary Parish Food Organizer.

If the worst happened!

minesweeping duties, and it is known that crew members would sometimes dispose of floating mines by shooting at them with rifles. Loss of life and limb were common, and families ashore were left with little to support them.

Miss Cubitt was salvage steward, collecting aluminium and paper: 'We want every scrap of paper, unwanted books and magazines!' Pulped paper was used as wadding around bullets.

In 1941 a 'Food Preservation Centre' was set up by Mrs Shillito at the rectory and Mrs Crowe at the Rookery, where jam was made using locally bought fruit. Villagers could sell small quantities to the centre, where Miss Last was chief jam maker – sugar was supplied to this and other such Women's Institute centres.

A meat pie scheme was set up at the Reading Room, and in the deanery magazine of September 1942 it was reported that:

Pies will be distributed once a week at the Reading Room between 3.30 and 4.30p.m. to those who have registered. Customers are asked to bring wrapping and cash, price 6d.

Nancy Mills remembers that they were 'made with whale meat and had goodness knows what else put in them, but they didn't need ration books and we liked them.'

From the deanery magazine:

Children kept safe till all clear goes. Members of the GFS are making pullovers, socks, sea boots, helmets, gloves and mittens, scarves, and handkerchiefs. In the event of the sirens sounding during a meeting the children will be kept in the Margaret Harker Hall until the 'All Clear' goes.

And in September 1940: 'The rainy weather during harvest may hinder both the incendiary bombs and the final in-gathering of the corn.'

Like other farmers and market gardeners, Mr Carter was in a reserved occupation. However, he joined the RAF in a 'hostilities only' capacity, which meant that he was demobbed after hostilities ended and came straight back to food production.

The Nicholls family had a Morrison shelter, which was like a big table with a bed underneath. Charlie Nicholls, his father and George Chapman went 'on watch' at the packing sheds down the road looking out for parachutes.

John Bulley recalls a morning when he was arriving at Hemblington School. He had just walked into the playground when he heard a plane coming over very low and firing. John, crouching under the hedge, looked up at the plane flying so low and close to him and wondered if he would be shot. When it had gone Mr Babbington, the headmaster, rushed outside and took him into school. The gunner, on his

way home, had been shooting at the glasshouses along Blofield Corner Road or Francis Lane.

Entries from Blofield School log-book during the war
September 1939: 'School admitted several children from evacuated areas.'
November 1939: 'Gas mask drill, children's respirators examined.' And in 1941:

School sports in connection with War Weapons Week – Major W. Harker presented each child with a 2/6 Saving Stamp.
School closed for Harvest Holiday. A talk on the danger of picking up dangerous objects was given to all children. Police Sergeant Bryer gave lecture & showed specimen of 'butterfly' and incendiary bombs to the whole school this afternoon.
Respirators examined – certain children went in gas van.

In 1944: 'Evacuee school at Margaret Harker Hall opened in September with 55 scholars from Dagenham, Essex.'
March 1945: 'Warned children re touching strange objects subsequent upon renewal of air raids.'

Many did valuable war work. Muriel Wright, later Read, and her friend, Marjorie Howes (later Barrett), hoped to join the forces but were asked instead to work in munitions. Muriel spent several years soldering parts for aeroplanes.

Evelyn Hanton joined the Army and spent three years during the war on the outskirts of London. She worked the 'predictors', to get the height and vertical and lateral details of bombers coming over, and passed the information to the gunners.

Those in reserved occupations had to join the ARP, police, ambulance or fire brigade.

The Home Guard
George Cann, the youngest in the Home Guard, was their runner, but ages ranged from 18 to 60. The volunteers met at the King's Head. 'You joined the Home Guard one week. The next week you got a rifle. Then they taught you how to use it.'

As a boy, Terry Starkings used to go down to Blofield turnpike and watch the Home Guard practise on the meadow where St Andrew's Way is now. He remembers a mortar gun shelling mock tanks.

When Baden Hanton was in the Home Guard Mr Golder was captain. They trained in the Margaret Harker Hall on Thursday evenings, and on Sundays, at Braydeston Hills or Strumpshaw gravel pits, there were manoeuvres and shooting practice. At the back of the King's Head car park was a little building where they took turns to do duty. 'The aim of the Home Guard,' says Baden, 'was to be able to scare the enemy off.'

Italian prisoners of war were based in Brundall

Blofield Home Guard, 1945. Left to right, back row: Kenny Smith, Ben Frost, Charlie Brady, Tom Dawson, Arthur Browne, ?, Fred Edrich, ?, George Bailey, Billy Brooks, Jimmy 'Brassy' Brown, ?, ?, Leonard Hubbard, Laddy Watson; third row: Ted Frost, ?, Mr Smith, Norman Marriott, Alfie Allen, ?, Cyril Trett, Percy Rope, Henry Bowring, ?, ?, Albert Francis, Claude Leeder, Jack Rope, Horace Howard, George Townsend; second row: ?, ?, Ernest Hanton, Herbert 'Winkle' Layt, Jack Land, Bertie Rope, Hedley Smith, Mr Golder, Mr Jack Gowing, ?, Bernard Read, ?, Harry Alden, ?, Fred Fountain, 'Bishy' Baynes, ?; front row: Arthur Knights, ?, Ben Richardson, Harry Rose, Walter Parker, George Cann, ?, Jack Marshall, Lenny Hayton, ?, Kenny 'Mucky' Hylton, Baden Hanton, Thomas Houghton, Cecil Parker, ?.

The Auxiliary Fire Service. On the right, back row: *George Forster;* fourth from left: *Stanley Trett;* front row, fourth from right: *Percy Skedge.*

The invasion committee, 1939–45. Left to right, back row: *?, Godfrey Weston, Mr W. Saunders, ?, Sergeant Bryar, Mr Park, Dr McKelvie;* front row: *Miss Ainsworth, Canon Shillito, Mr Saunders, Major Harker, Dr Deacon, Mr Palmer, Mr Martin.*

The first aid post, c.1940. Left to right, back row: ?, Mrs Kahler, Eva Marshall; front row: Eileen Rogers, Miss Cubitt, Jean Bailey.

and worked on several local farms. Chris Basey recalls that:

They seemed to have plenty of freedom and I can remember how, in the evenings, they used to walk up

and down the Street and Highfield Avenue doing their 'passeggiata' as they would have done at home.

Notes from the deanery magazine:
Church bells were silenced. During the blackout the 6.30 service was brought forward to 6.0p.m.

September 1940, News of our men:
A Memorial service for leading signalman Richard Beck was held on Sunday 4 August. As a boy he was in the church choir and won Chamberlin prizes on four occasions.

Frank Ward has had a shaking in an air raid, and has been home on leave.

Jack King, aged 19½, was badly injured as a civilian in a recent air raid; it has been found necessary to amputate a leg. His many friends are distressed for him.

The good women of our parish are getting ready with Christmas gifts and comforts for local defence units.

From the notes of a member of the ambulance group.

In June 1940 the County Council provided a trailer ambulance and a sitting case car, these were kept at Mrs Blofield's Lound Lodge. Members were invited to volunteer for night duty in the loft above the stables where the cars were kept. In company with rats, black beetles, spiders and other specimens…

In October the County Council commandeered the Infant Welfare Room at the Margaret Harker Hall and evening duty from 5.30p.m.–9.30p.m. was undertaken by the ladies with one all night duty a week, the other nights being undertaken by the men.

The ambulance and ARP group in the 1940s. Those on ambulance duty would sleep in the Red Cross hut. Left to right, back row: Mr Cann, ?, ?, Leslie Baynes, ?, Mr Saunders, Mrs Hall, Ruby Stone, Miss Cubitt, ?, ?, ?, ?; middle row: George Willimott, Mr Kahler, ?, Mr W. Saunders, Miss Owls, Mr Howes, Dr Steele, ?, ?, ?, Ben Hanton; front row: Miss Taylor, Evelyn Woods, Helen Grass, Daisy Bussey, Mrs Turner.

Convalescent home at Blofield Hall, c.1944. Among those pictured are left to right, third row: Ray Walker (patient), VAD Nurses Jude, Benns (later Place), Hammond and Middleton (who married Ray Walker); second row, centre: Sister; front row, sixth from left: a Polish airman.

April 1942:

Don't let us forget the men from this parish in Singapore and our missionaries in Singapore, Hong Kong, Rangoon and Sarawak. We are learning geography as never before, and this should develop in us the habit of loving intercession.

Church Flag Staff
The Church Council has just accepted the generous offer of a flag staff to be erected on the church tower with a suitable flag, in readiness for the happy day when victory and peace arrives.

Welcome Home Fund
The committee has decided to reserve the decision of the form of welcome until such time as a sufficient number of men and women have returned from war service. The fund has grown to £250.

After the Second World War, the following names were added to the war memorial:

1939–45

Benjamin Barber	Ronald Hylton
Richard Beck	Leonard Marshall
Walter Beck	Ronnie Marshall
Reggie Bussey	John Spooner
Matthew Hanton	Stanley Trett
Harold High	George Weston
Cyril Hylton	Godfrey Weston

A book of remembrance, planned for Blofield Church, will give details of the lives and deaths of those Blofield men who gave their lives in the two world wars.

The wedding at Mallett's Farm on 10 October 1898 of Alice Reynolds and John Culyer. Standing at extreme back: the Downs boys; left to right, back row: ?, ?, ?, ?, John Culyer (leather merchant), ?, Eva Downs, ?, Harry Downs, Alice Weston, Godfrey Weston, Sophia Reynolds; front, seated: ?, ?, ?, ?, John Culyer (groom), Alice Jane Reynolds (bride), Joshua Reynolds, Trinny Reynolds, Emily Weston; seated on ground: ?, ?, Karen Reynolds, Grace Mary Weston.

A morphory (converted tumbril) at Mallett's Farm, c.1935. Left to right: Ernest Kipper, Charles Howes, Marjorie Howes, Maud Howes, Joan Balls.

CHAPTER 7

Farming

After about 1500 this fertile peninsula of land between two rivers became concerned primarily with arable farming. More recently it has been important as a market gardening centre.

Many of the old family names of farmers and market gardeners survive in the area today, often in the names of lokes and lanes.

Smallholdings

Around the turn of the nineteenth century moves had been made towards making allotments and smallholdings more available to farm labourers.

Henry J. Waters, from Freethorpe, whose son Wilfrid later married Grace Weston of Gables Farm, had long been an exponent of the idea that land should be available to ordinary country folk.

For years farmers were bitterly opposed to allotments and smallholdings. Their view was that labourers were born as labourers. They used to ask why the labourers should take land that ought to go to farmers' sons and nephews. I was one who led the call for land for allotments and smallholdings.

Following the First World War the government, seeking to help returning ex-servicemen, passed the Smallholding Colonies (Amendment) Act of 1918, enabling local authorities to borrow money for the purchase of land to be let to these men.

Early in 1919 some 3,000 ex-soldiers, working on various farms, were contacted and 500 of them applied for land to rent. The extensive Burlingham Hall Estate happened to come up for auction at this time. Its owner, Mr Burroughes, threatened with compulsory purchase, agreed to sell a substantial area of the estate privately to the County Council, and 3,000 acres were withdrawn from the auction.

Angry landowner and angry tenants

This angered Mr Burroughes, who had hoped his tenants would have an opportunity to buy. It also angered the tenants who, having made arrangements to bid for their farms, were only told by the auctioneer on the day of the sale that many lots had been withdrawn. They were understandably disappointed.

At the sale, at the Agricultural Hall in Norwich, on Friday, 1 August 1919, the council paid £312,500 for 3,087 acres of land, together with all farmhouses buildings and cottages.

Although most of the tenancies were transferred, some farms were divided into smallholdings of about four to 20 acres to be let to ex-servicemen. Accommodation for tenants and their families was initially provided at Burlingham House until the Council purchased wooden huts.

Early difficulties

In the early years life was difficult for the tenants, many of whom had no knowledge of the land, animals or cultivation. Even those who had knowledge found it hard to make a living on such small plots. Many had to give up and the 'moonlight flit' – leaving in an 'unsatisfactory manner, surreptitiously, late at night'– was a common occurrence.

Over the years acreage was increased to make the smallholdings viable and bungalows were built to accommodate the new farmers. Plots of about 30–50 acres enabled a man to support his family with, typically, a cow, some chickens and crops.

They grew corn, mangolds and perhaps sugar beet, a relatively new crop. The sugar beet factory at Cantley had opened in 1912 and many men returning from the war found employment here.

The Smallholdings in These Parishes

By 1937 Mallett's Farm in Holly Lane had two smallholdings, where Walter Ball and Charles Howes had land. In Bullacebush Lane were another two, with Bertie and Frank Rope, followed later by Gerald Basey-Fisher. At Perowne's Farm were Mr Jermy and George Basey-Fisher. George's son, nicknamed Did, later followed him into Perowne's Farm. Sparrow Hall was one smallholding with the Wheelhouse family and then the Fullers. Highnoon Farm in Hemblington had the Saunders brothers and the Moores, later Hearn and Locke, and the land down the school loke in Mill Road was farmed by Mr Bulley.

Mallett's Farm

Before it became smallholdings Mr Joshua Reynolds held Mallett's Farm. His daughter was married from here in 1898.

Charlie Howes grew up and learned farming from his father, Charles, on this 39-acre smallholding.

Nearly all smallholdings had a few cows. Lorries from the Milk Marketing Board came round to collect milk in churns from each farm. Olive Richards (née Howes) remembers that her mother, Maud, used

Mallett's barn, dated 1659 and admired by Pevsner, was demolished c.1984 by the County Council Farms department.

The Basey-Fisher family, 1931. Left to right, standing: Peter, Elizabeth, Frances, George; front row: George, Betty, Leslie.

some of the milk to make butter:

'A scheme in 1960s wanted little people to give up milk and we were paid £300 a cow to give up,' said Charlie.

Perowne's Farm

Perowne's Farm in Bullacebush Lane was owned in 1851 by William Perowne. Mr George Robert Basey-Fisher and his wife Frances moved there from Ashby St Mary in October 1921, and he farmed there until his death in 1975.

Their son George, known to many as Did, was born at Ashby, the other children Leslie, Betty and Gerald being born at Blofield.

Gerald remembers that, as a 10-year-old , he saw 11 pairs of horses ploughing on Sutton's field opposite Minns Farm. This was two-furrow ploughing; in those days three or four horses would pull a binder.

Leslie Basey-Fisher was used to horses on the farm where he grew up:

George, Uncle Albert and George junr (Did), c.1939.

On a visit to Ashby, to my father's family, the horse and cart drove on to the Reedham chain ferry. The horse got a wasp in its ear and caused quite a commotion when it reared up during the river crossing.

The Milk Marketing Board in St Stephens Street in Norwich was the distribution centre for bottled milk. Leslie worked there until 1945 and then took on the school milk round for Norfolk. He and his wife, Daphne, covered 200 miles a day using two vans, driving from 5a.m. to 11.30a.m. each day and delivering to every school in Norwich and the county.

For 40 years of their married life they lived in Lower Globe Lane with views of Rope's orchards and market gardens.

Leslie's mother taught Daphne how to make

Gerald, Did and George with their first tractor, c.1941.

'On the Spot' service, 1942.

Jack Wheelhouse, Leslie and Did with George (seated), *c.1939.*

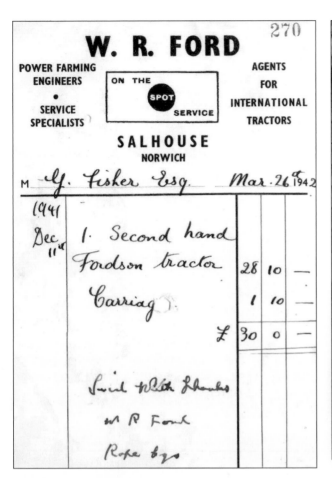

Leslie, Glenna Rope and Gerald, c.1940.

Gerald Basey-Fisher covering sugar beet, 1951.

and fattening pigs. Their crops were sugar beet, wheat, barley and peas for Birds Eye.

botanic beer, a real old farmer's drink for harvest time – good and thirst quenching.

Sparrow Hall
The Wheelhouse family were at Sparrow Hall before the war and later Tom Fuller farmed here until he retired in the mid-1970s.

Ernest Morse, the rose grower, had land in Eaton, Brundall and also some at Sparrow Hall. During the Second World War his Sparrow Hall fields were requisitioned for the production of food.

Bullacebush Farm
From 1969 to 1998, Gerald and Janet Basey-Fisher farmed at Bullacebush, keeping cattle and breeding

Tom Fuller at Sparrow Hall during harvest, c.1946. Left to right: Billy Trett, Tom, with his daughter Pat, Brian and Nancy (on the horse) and Dougie Adams.

Bullocks with High Gallows plough at High Noon Farm, 1895. Godfrey Weston is watching and Moke Marjoram rides one bullock.

Henry Locke moved to High Noon and farmed for some years. Nowadays, their son Michael keeps 200 lambing ewes and has 100 cattle, which he grazes on the Acle and Upton marshes.

Market Gardens

Blofield and Hemblington has long been an area of orchards, soft fruit and flower production.

Throughout the first half of the twentieth century Blofield Heath was a busy area, with many people growing produce and working together to transport it by carts, vans or lorries to market at Acle, Norwich, London and, in the case of cut flowers, to markets further afield.

Morse's fields, c.1945. As the self binder worked, the ever-diminishing cornfield produced a good catch of rabbits
Left to right: *?, Ernest Morse, George Forster, Bob Nobbs, Fred Parker, ?, ?, Jack Stone, Eben Mayes, Tim Worrall (child), ?, Sybil Nobbs, Arthur Knights, ?, Fred Morse, ?, ?, ?, Desmond Gibbs, ?.*

High Noon Farm

The Saunders brothers were at High Noon Farm and by 1937 Leslie Moore was also farming there. Later it was farmed by Peter Hearn and in 1961 Margaret and

Mike Nicholls

Six generations of the Nicholls family have lived at Sawley Villa in Blofield Corner Road, working for some years as market gardeners growing flowers and soft fruit. Mike's great-grandmother, Eliza Ellingham, was the first official flower seller on Norwich market. Her family had been in Blofield since the seventeenth century.

Chrysanthemums and other cut flowers went from Brundall Station every day to Covent Garden. An early morning train which stopped at all stations from Yarmouth through to Norwich, collecting produce for London markets, continued to run until the early 1950s.

Bulbs such as daffodils, narcissi and tulips from Holland were grown, as were gooseberries, raspberries, strawberries and blackcurrants.

Tomatoes grew in large greenhouses heated by a hot water system run by coke boilers. Grandfather Nicholls dug out huge storage tanks to collect rainwater from all the corrugated iron roofs. He watered the plants while grandmother worked the pump!

As in many other households, drinking water

High Noon Farm, Hemblington, c.1970.

Charlie and Millicent Nicholls, William and Ernie picking tomatoes, c.1930.

The yard at Sawley Villa in 1925. William was a haulage contractor until 1948.

William Nicholls, 1918. This horse would bring William home from Norwich when he fell asleep at the reins.

Charles, in front of the packing sheds at Sawley Villa, c.1924.

came from a well sunk by Gedge the builders. When Mike first remembers the house in the 1940s there was no electricity and no running water. The toilet stood at the top of garden. Night soil was not collected; you dug a trench and emptied it in.

His grandfather planted a row of 24 variegated holly trees whose foliage was cut to make Christmas decorations and wreaths for funerals.

A horse and cart took produce to the early morning wholesale market on the old cattle market, and his grandfather took the horse and cart to Norwich twice a week. His father, 14 or 15 at the time, would go with him. Grandfather would take a bicycle and cycle back, as it was quicker, leaving father to return with the horse and cart. Several times he fell asleep coming home and woke up in the yard, as the horse knew its own way back.

The most frightening thing was meeting the mail coach as it came down Postwick Hill having changed horses at Witton:

You just got out of the way because they were going like the clappers. They changed horses at Witton, Acle and Yarmouth.

Father was a haulage contractor. He bought three or four lorries and would cart anything.

When carting sugar beet it could be quite frightening going to Cantley because the road there was very

narrow. The worst lorries to pass were steam-driven lorries. The only way they could pass was to drive as if on collision course straight and then, at the last minute, steer round each other.

Albert Francis, after whom Francis Loke is named, also took produce to market. He had a lorry and collected chrysanthemums, tomatoes, daffodils – whatever produce people had – to take to market in Acle or Norwich.

Albert's son, Jimmy, recalls:

In the early days I would go with my father to the wholesale green grocery market, where the Mall is. I've stood on there at 4 o'clock on a Friday morning helping to sell the goods we had collected around the village. By Saturday they had put all the cattle things back.

The peach house at The Heath end of Francis Lane, c.1978.

The Neave smallholding, 1960s.

Sisters **Anne Ashington and Julia Carter** remember that their grandfather's family settled at Blofield Heath as market gardeners. The Carters' family house, called The Heath, was at the end of Francis Lane. Their grandfather pulled up the trees from an orchard there and began to erect glasshouses to grow tomatoes.

Their water came from an artesian well which was very deep – they needed a good supply to water the plants. It was lovely, cold water to drink, and one or two mothers would come to get water to mix baby formula as it was so pure and free of nitrates.

They grew chrysanthemums outside, bringing them inside to flower for Christmas. They also grew snapdragons, stocks and daffodils – old daffodil bulbs were often dumped at a field edge and some nice old varieties can be seen growing in verges even now!

The chrysanthemums went to Liverpool, Manchester and Birmingham, as well as to Covent Garden in London. Grown for the Christmas trade, they were sent by railway lorry to the station in order to reach their destination by Christmas Eve, as this was when people expected to buy their flowers.

Transport had to be quick and reliable as flowers which were left in cold conditions would be frosted and turn brown.

Other produce they grew were beans, cucumbers, lettuce and radishes.

Initially, a railway lorry took produce to Brundall Station three times a week, but later the carrier went straight to Norwich Station.

Working for the Carters were Daisy Norton, who was a land girl, Bob Griffin and his wife, the Chapmans and Ann Chipperfield. The men were permanent staff, while the women were usually seasonal workers, helping with picking and packing.

The Bunns grew tomatoes in six greenhouses opposite the recreation ground, where Rosemary Road is now. They were sold locally but lorry loads also went to Covent Garden for the Easter weekend.

The holding in Dyes Road was first Earl's, then Youngman's, followed by Wheelhouse, then Neave, followed by the SHES (Sheltered Horticultural Employment Scheme.)

John Bulley recalls that 'that little crossroads at Dyes Road and Bonds Road was always known as Earl's Corner.'

When **David and Phyllis Neave** had this holding they grew vegetables and fruit. In their early married years they had a motor bike to which, when the first child arrived, a sidecar was added. To accommodate the second child this became a double sidecar and when number three came on the scene Phyllis and David acquired an Army truck. The final venture was a family car!

Their's was a busy life. They kept 50 chickens and grew sugar beet. So that they could work at night when the children were in bed, they rigged up lights and worked until midnight, topping and tailing the beets.

Another venture was bee-keeping, for which Mr Chipperfield, an expert bee-keeper, taught David and Phyllis the necessary skills.

Phyllis tells the story of a swarm of bees they were asked to remove from under the eaves of a chip shop in Wroxham. David and his son-in-law, John Spinks, waited until after dark, as that is the best time to deal with bees, and appeared, clad in their all-enveloping white outfits, much to the surprise of the queue of hungry holiday-makers waiting for their fish and chips. David and John took off the eave timbers, removed the bees and brought them back to a hive at the top of their holding. Next morning, when they went to have a look, the bees had gone. They knew bees would fly up to two and a half miles, but these had flown more than four miles back to Wroxham and were happily under the eaves again!

SHES, which now occupies Heath End Farm, provides a range of activities for the disabled and for those in special care or with special needs, affording them contact with those who come to buy plants, eggs and vegetables.

On six acres of grassland there are greenhouses and domestic animals ranging from free-range chickens and pigmy goats to rabbits and Shetland ponies.

Nurseries – 'the Dutchman's Fields'

Mr Ellerbrook, the son of an award-winning rose grower of Booksop, in Holland, came with his wife to Norfolk in 1938, initially growing roses at The Willows in Upton. When the war came he put his land down to vegetables to boost wartime food production, and in 1946 the couple settled in Blofield, where they bought land from the Edrichs.

Adept at building up from scratch, Mr Ellerbrook constructed glasshouses, forming the concrete beams and cladding them with timber from the blitz. He even bought redundant submarine boiler pipes to use as heating pipes in the glasshouses. Working long hours and being thrifty with all materials, he passed on these values to his staff.

Mrs Eileen Goldsmith (née Bickers) recalls:

He never threw away a piece of string or a rubber band. His wife sat indoors and made all the coloured labels for the plants. The Ellerbrooks always spoke to you. He was the best boss I ever had and his wife was a lady.

Gradually, a thriving business grew. In the 1960s, Eileen's early days working there, the busiest time was when they prepared the azaleas and Christmas roses for Mothering Sunday. Michael Ellerbrook recalls that his father experimented, growing 'a

Ellerbrook's staff in 1962. Left to right at back: *Marjorie Cann, Cath Barber;* front: *Vi Bickers, Beryl Mackerell.*

cracking good crop of outdoor tomatoes' and selling onions by mail order.

Soon such pot plants as azaleas, rhododendrons and camelias were being dispatched to 1,100 branches of F.W. Woolworth and up to 22 staff were employed in the packing sheds.

In 1970 the business moved to Hall Road where, in 2006, cuttings are prepared for sale to other nurseries.

Four generation of Ellerbrooks have been nurserymen, with Michael and John Paul taking the business into the future.

Farms

Gables Farm, Hemblington
The area of land farmed by the Westons at Gables Farm constituted a third of the area of the parish.

Nathaniel Weston (1749–1874) bought Gables Farm in 1832. The small notebook he kept, entitled '1837 Map of my Farm at Hemblington', lists such field names as 'Starlings, Doveshouse Close, Carr Close, Fishpond Close, Smiths Pitle and Old Raggs.'

In 1873 his chief horseman was Horman, who reached the age of 100, as did his wife. Charlotte, their daughter, was a milkmaid for 50 years.

Gables Farm passed to Nat's great-nephew, Godfrey William Weston (1849–1927). His son, another Godfrey, born in 1883, eventually took over

Mr Ellerbrook, c.1961.

Gables Farm, 1873. Left to right: *Horman (chief horseman), Mrs Godfrey Weston, Edward Baynes, Charlotte, Godfrey Weston, Jimmy Dye (bullock feeder).*

the farm, retiring in 1960. His six siblings included George, who went to New Zealand, and a sister, Alice, who joined the Red Cross and worked as a Voluntary Aid Detachment nurse under Margaret Harker at Brundall war hospital during the First World War. She did much to help in Hemblington church and was the organist there.

In the deanery magazine for November 1918, Revd A. Shillito wrote of Miss Alice Weston: 'We all congratulate Mr Minchin on winning Miss Weston as his bride; but we scarcely know what we shall do without her.'

It was another sister, Grace, who married Wilfrid Waters, son of Henry J. Waters from Freethorpe, who

Gables Farm, 1873. Left to right: *Charlotte (dairy maid) and her father Horman, Edward Baynes, Nathaniel Weston, Mrs Godfrey Weston, Godfrey Weston.*

Gables Farm, c.1910.

Gables Farm, 1932.

promoted the concept of smallholdings.

Grace and Wilfrid's son, Jim, now 80, remembers boyhood summer holidays at Gables Farm and his grandfather, Godfrey Weston:

Each year Godfrey went to Ireland to meet a dealer who collected his type of 2–2½ year old bullocks to fatten. These were shipped over to England, where they were grazed during the summer on Acle marshes. On these marshes would be a man living there named a 'Looker'. It was his job to see if there were any cattle which did not look right. He would then inform the owner. In the early autumn the cattle were brought back to the farm to be fattened. They were fed on barley straw, mangolds

and seed cake. This cake came in slabs which were fed into a machine and I helped turn the handle to break it up. In the spring, when the cattle had been sold, the yards were mucked out and the manure was stored in a big heap until it was spread. He told me the muck was what he wanted and sometimes he did not make much money on the bullocks.

My father delivered us in his model T Ford to Gables Farm each summer for a week's holiday and then drove straight home as he was a veterinary surgeon working on his own.

The lighting in the house was by oil-lamps and I took a candle when going to bed. On a Saturday night I would have a bath in a tin bath in the kitchen, the water

Threshing at Gables Farm, 1920. Left to right: *Arthur Barber, ?, Albert Barber, Jack Middleton, Russell Mayer, Eileen Mayer, Louis Hylton, Jack Thompson, Sam Mayer, ?.*

Harvest at Hemblington, c.1920. **Left to right:** *Nellie Barber, Arthur Barber, Albert Barber, ? Groves, Jack Middleton, Louis Hylton, ?.*

being heated on the stove. My aunt Marjorie baked a loaf of unleavened bread and cut it in small pieces for communion on Sundays. Opposite the back door was the wash house, in which there was always a cauldron of hot water hanging over the fire. In the next room was the dairy where my aunt made the butter. I always liked to help her. She had special pats for making patterns on the butter.

Across the garden were the horse yard and stables. Godfrey was very proud of his Percheron horses. When he had been to a circus he taught his horses to lie down. Unfortunately, one day he went into the stable, touched the horse's side and it rolled over on top of him, breaking some of his ribs.

At the far end of the garden were the privies. The soil was taken into the orchard twice a year. The toilet paper

Stack building Hemblington, c.1920. **Left to right:** *Louis Hylton, Jack Thompson, ?, Albert Barber, ?, Jimmy Bidewell.*

Godfrey Weston and Harper inspecting crops, 1930.

Harvesting, 1939. Godfrey Weston with Kenny Hylton driving a Case tractor on Long Piece.

Gables Low Barn, c.1938. If you kept horses it took one third of the farm to feed them.

Walter the stockman at Gables Farm, 1910.

was pages from the Farm and Stockman *magazine.*

On the other side of the road opposite the washhouse was a field called the Bleach because in the olden days sheets were laid out in the sun.

Down the loke at the back of the farmyard I used to help the men drive the fat bullocks to Acle market. I would run ahead and stand in any open gateway till we joined the road known as the Turnpike. The men would walk back from Acle but I got a lift in my uncle's car.

On the road to Pedham was the Lower Barn and yard which was used for the fattening of bullocks. There were some cottages nearby and I believe this is where Walter the stockman lived.

Only three or four out of a group of ten bullocks could be trained to pull the plough. Teams were slow and needed to be worked by older men who were patient with them. When harrowing or rolling they would do as much as a horse so long as they were worked round and round the field and would plod on for hours, whereas a horse, working up and down a field, wanted a breather at each end.

Bullocks worked till they were eight or nine and then were fattened for market. Teams continued to be used until about 1904.

Godfrey may have cherished hopes that one or both of his nephews, Godfrey and George, might eventually succeed him in farming at Hemblington, but these hopes were dashed by their tragic deaths in the war. Members of the New Zealand Airforce, they both died flying from bases within the UK and are buried side by side to the west of the round tower of Hemblington Church.

Christopher and Jean Wace came to Gables Farm in 1960 following Godfrey's retirement.

Their farming was mixed arable – sugar beet, wheat and potatoes, with beans and peas being grown for Birds Eye and horseradish and mint for Colmans. In the 1970s Christopher had 30 acres of strawberries and 15 acres of blackcurrants. Allowing the public to pick the remaining fruit after the main picking was the beginning of their 'pick your own' (PYO) scheme. Many varieties of vegetable and fruit were grown in the 1980s on the Yarmouth Road beside Brewster Court, where Smith and Wace PYO was popular.

Terry Starkings

When the Burroughes Estate came up for sale in 1919 Terry's grandfather, Alfred John Youngs, bought Hemblington Hall with 333 acres, 10 cottages and a blacksmith's shop. It cost him £9,250:

You can see where four of the cottages and a blacksmith's forge stood on Hemblington Hill. The cottage had a box hedge and a path up to the door. Several plants growing on the roadside verge are escapees from the old cottage gardens.

When Grandfather retired to The Croft he put his daughter Beulah and her husband, Jack Cutler, into the front of Hemblington Hall, Margery and Leslie Moore in the back, another daughter Ella at Hickling and another, Daisy, at Wood Farm.

Terry's father owned a bull-nosed Morris Cowley, with a dickey seat at the back, which he had adapted to carry churns to the Milk Marketing Board in St Stephens, bringing back school milk in crates. By the time he came to Wood Farm in 1945 tankers were coming round to collect milk churns from each farm. The car, also known as a doctor's coupé, ended its life as a milk float! At that time the sugar beet was moved in steam lorries with solid tyres.

Terry and his son, Gary, now farm the 122 acres at Wood Farm.

Phyllis Jermy (née Cutler), granddaughter of John Youngs of Hemblington Hall, was born in 1920 in a cottage in Hemblington Hill next to the blacksmith's shop.

Grandfather Youngs took us occasionally in his car to the Norwich cattle market. Nanny went every week and sometimes asked one of us girls to go. She would go into Lyons and buy us an ice cream. We thought that was marvellous. When we came out along Ber Street there used to be all herds of bullocks and we would drive through them.

I remember once coming home from the Agricultural show there was what they call a 'pea souper' that was as thick as a hedge. Someone had to walk in front of the car to see where the side of the road was, that was so thick. The show was October or November time of the year at the Agricultural hall.

There was hardly a time when it wasn't foggy at the show time. I used to like going because there was a fair up there. That was our thing, never mind about the bullocks. Grandad won a lot of prizes. He had a whole wall full of first and second prizes.

Mother and Dad gave us the farm in 1968 or '69 and we've been here ever since.

Phyllis's son Rex now farms the land. Phyllis did:

... all the tractor driving and all the ploughing and I have done it up to a little while ago. But I daren't tackle it now; the tractors have got too technical. It's push this and push that so I don't know what to do now though I could get one down the road behind Rex if he needs me.

Eric and Ron Dawson are cousins whose fathers farmed at Walnut Tree Farm on Blofield Corner Road. Eric recounts:

Grandfather was a shoemaker on Blofield Corner. People then had allotments, one acre each, and grew

Harry Ling with cottages and the blacksmith shop in the background, c.1946.

Eric Dawson, his father Sidney, Ron and his father, Edward, 1980.

vegetables. Grandmother went to Norwich with the pony and cart to sell the produce.

Father said she used to tie up the horse at the bottom of St Stephens and since then, when I've taken him up to Norwich, he thought we ought to stop the car there.

Well, we'd be out in the yard and hear Grandmother's pony trotting back past Plumstead school and the dog would run out to meet her. There was no traffic on the road then and it was that quiet.

On the holding beside the house they grew fruit and took it to Norwich to the Haymarket, initially with a horse and cart, later in a model T Ford left-hand-drive lorry.

As boys we had a marvellous time because we had everything we wanted. We had horses. My father lifted me on a horse about 18 months old. We always had a horse to ride and a field to play football on so we were never bored.

There were four horses on a binder during the war. Ronnie would ride the front one and Eric the one at the back. They were right in the country then, with trees right up to the top of the road and orchards all around.

On the farm they had 80 acres, with arable, pigs and cattle. It was hard manual work, walking up and down the field every day.

John Bulley's grandfather was a pork butcher in Mill Road and they kept their own pigs. As a boy John used to turn the handle to crank out the sausages: 'The slaughterhouse was behind and there were pig sheds and a barn. We used to deliver with a pony and trap all round Blofield.' The butchery business closed at the outbreak of the war.

Leaving school at 14, John worked for his grandfather on his smallholding. John's father then had a County Council smallholding down the school loke. Here John worked, first for his father Wilfred until

John Bulley, 2006, with tools used in sugar beet harvesting. The plough was last used in the winter of 1962/63, when the ground was frozen too hard for any other plough.

he retired, and now for Derek Bond, to whom Wilfred sold the land. 'I've been on the land all my life,' says John.

Derek Bond's father bought Heath Farm in 1920 and began by farming corn, mangolds and hay and keeping bullocks and just two or three suckling cows.

The 1960s saw a swing to peas and dwarf beans for Birds Eye, followed by the introduction of parsley, mint and horseradish grown for Colmans.

Derek's son, David, introduced bulb growing, with 15 varieties of daffodils, the bulbs being harvested from June onwards, dried for three weeks and graded for size, the big ones being sold and the small ones planted again.

By the mid-1990s sugar beet, corn and some set-

Cutting the corn in Bond's field, 1930s.

Harvesting horseradish at Heath Farm, 2005.

Cottages on Bonds Road.

Heath Farm haystacks, photographed by Edward Lincoln Helsdon (of Dove Cottage) in 1938.

aside were joined by tarragon and rosemary. As these crops need hand weeding to reduce the need for spraying, the work force is kept busy and there are several harvests a year.

Mary Oliver (née Bond) grew up at Heath Farm:

Saturday was cattle market day. Father liked to see what other farmers were selling in Norwich so on Saturdays he went along. At the Corn hall he would negotiate a good price for his corn or buy seed corn or fertiliser.

When Mary was a girl they had four horses:

George was the team man for the horses and also the stacker. I loved to get up early to talk to George. I would sit on the edge of the manger and stroke the horses while they were having their oats or chaff.

George was skilled at stack building. Hedge trimmings were spread in a circle on the ground in the stackyard where the stack was to be built. This kept a movement of air under the stack to keep the corn dry. The sheaves of corn were placed butt end out from centre to edge of the circle, continuing upwards till the stack reached the correct height, when it began to be shaped inwards to create a sloping top. This was thatched with wheat straw to keep out the rain.

In the school holidays Mary used to drive the tractor and would be turned loose in a 10-acre field to pull the charlock (a yellow flowered weed) so that it wasn't caught up and seeded again at harvest time:

You would pull it up, get an arm full of it, walk to the end of the field dump it in the hedgerow walk back to where you had been and start all over again. Another job was thistles. We had a spud like an outsized crochet hook only with the inner edge sharp. You cut through the thistle stem. I did that with great enthusiasm because any I missed at that point I would be sure to

find when I picked up the sheaves to put on the stook. You cut docks with a spud as well.

To earn pocket money she was allowed to pick mushrooms. She would put them in a basket and a local smallholder would take them to market and bring her back some pocket money. One year she picked sackfuls of acorns to sell to a neighbouring farmer who kept pigs.

During the depression of the late 20s in early 30s:

... money was probably not flowing all that freely in the farming community and 6d. a week pocket money was a fortune. If I had between 2d. and 6d. I thought I owned the world.

It was a wonderful place to grow up. As we looked across from the farm it was all orchards and gardens.

Tony Rope's grandfather, Stephen, came to Street Farm in 1897 and planted up the orchard. His brother, Billy, went the other side of the main road and planted an orchard which was later worked by his son, Percy.

Tony's parents went up to Bullacebush Road in 1924 and ran the holding with Stephen, who liked to do the orchard work. This is where Tony was born in November 1925, when the snow was lying deep and had blocked some roads. He tells the story: 'Dr McKelvie and the district nurse had to walk across the footpath because they couldn't get up Plantation Road. The snow was all drifted into the road.'

Old Ted Vann later told Tony, 'Your father came across and said "that's a boy" and I said "poor little soul coming into a cold, white world like this."'

Grandfather Stephen bought Church Farm and land behind the Turret House loke and Manor Ridge.

'We had horses working in the orchard, one horse here at Street farm and five down at Church Farm.'

The Street Farm cows used to walk down the pathway to a field past the school. The footpath was always softer: 'If the cows walked along the main road stones would go into their hooves, so they'd walk all the way down on the path.'

Pick your own became popular in the 1980s. In the early 1970s, when Tony had lots of raspberries left unpicked at Street Farm, he suggested letting the public pick their own. His father was very sceptical, but Tony went ahead and advertised 'Pick your own and picnic in a hayfield.'

It was so popular that Tony had to go and get Abiathar Jermy to help him, and at the end of the day Frank conceded that there wasn't a raspberry left. The fruit grew where Edrich Close is now. When the Street Farm land was sold for housing Tony grew several acres of soft fruit on the land at the end of the Turret House loke and PYO signs went up there.

Dawlings Farm was originally part of the Blofield Hall Estate and when Eric Butler bought it in 1951 it had a cow, chickens and pigs. Glenna Butler explains

The Rope family at Street Farm, c.1919. Left to right, back row: *Frank, Jack, Elsie, Donald, Bertie;* front row: *Archie, Stephen, Sarah, George.*

The model T Ford truck loaded and ready for market, late 1920s. Frank Rope is in the centre.

Ted Vann and his wife having their 'fourses'.

The Rope family on the occasion of Donald's visit from Canada, c.1949. Left to right: Jack, George, Bertie, Elsie, Donald, Frank and Archie.

that by the 1960s deep litter hens were in the barn and pullets on the low meadows. Next came a change to 30 cows, fed from cut grass in mangers rather than grazing before they were turned out into the woods and low meadows. Milking three times a day was tried for a while.

The idea of pick your own at Dawlings Farm started with a few raspberries in 1973 and escalated rapidly until there were 25 acres with a wide variety of fruits for the public to pick in delightful surroundings.

The public were soon beating a path to Blofield in the summer.

Rope's harvest, 1952. Left to right, back row: George Moore, Gillian Rope, Joyce Franklin, ?, ?; middle row: Tony Rope, Roger Rope, Stephen Rope, Dennis 'Tich' Buckland; front row: Vera Buckland (née Bugden), Charlie Edrich, Archie Rope.

Farming Traditions

A harvest-time custom was described by Peter Eade, whose father was Blofield's doctor from 1825 to 1860:

It was at this time common for harvest-men, at the conclusion of harvest, to call upon the doctor and other connections of their employer and ask for 'largesse'. I can well remember many of these parties coming from various parishes and assembling upon the lawn in front of my father's house, when, after receiving a harvest gift, they would all form in a circle and 'holler (halloa) largess' lustily. Later on this custom was largely replaced by the farmer giving his men and their wives, etc., a harvest supper at his own house, followed by a dance, in which his family and some invited friends would join.

Mr Myrus Sutton was a big local landowner with a farm at Panxworth, another at Upton, two at Freethorpe and one at Halvergate. Minns Farm and the farm in Field Lane also belonged to him. Here Mr Charles Skedge used to be Sutton's foreman and

Charles Skedge, foreman at Field Lane Farm, 1938.

Myrus Sutton's farm in Field Lane, 6 December 1956. Left to right: two horses Prince and Bonny, Eric Hammond, Tom Clarke, Bridget (horse), Kitty (horse), Brian Francis, Bob Newstead, Reginald Garwood.

went round with a pony and trap.

In 2002 Clifford 'Jimmy' Francis recounted his farming experiences with Myrus Sutton. Growing up at the Orchard Market Garden, where Borton Road is now, Jimmy went to work for Mr Sutton in 1959 when he was 15:

Suttons at Blofield were one of the last places to use horses in any great numbers. There were eight horses and when I started the horses did the drilling, harrowing and horse hoeing of the sugar beet. The horses knew you. If they were wary their ears would go back. If they liked you you could get them to do almost anything. Old Tom Clark could get a horse to do anything. He was a good horse man. He taught me how to plough with a horse.

Every horse had its own harness and its own collar to fit its neck. There was a harness room and the harness had to be oiled and looked after. If you sold a horse its harness would go with it. New collars etc would be made by the harness maker. Halters could be altered to fit any horse but the collar was individual and had to fit.

The saddle was made to take the back chain. There was what they called a 'tree' on top; a piece of wood with a large groove in it which the back chain went over, and to hold it on there would be the belly strap.

Some of the horses you could ride. Some of them you couldn't sit on the saddle they'd just propel you in the air and just wouldn't wear it. You needed a thick corn sack or you'd get sweat rash off the horse.

In harvest time the 'hold ye' boy would ride on them with an old sack put over the wooden part of the saddle, and would sit between that and the neck of the horse with a leading rein in his hand.

They called him 'hold ye' because every time, before he moved the horse, he would have to call out, 'Hold' for the man on top of the wagon who was loading the shooves, so he was aware that you were going to move or he would be off the back. And he would call out 'gee' to the horse to tell it to move.

The horses were heavy horses, Suffolks.

There were stables and a barn, bullock sheds and yards, horse yards, which are now all turned into houses in Field Lane.

A tumbrel was a small two-wheeled cart the horse had to support. Tumbrels gradually sloped to the back so you couldn't put too much on the back.

They were used for carting muck, sugar beet and tops. It had to be carefully loaded. We had one old horse she was ever so slow but when she moved forward she'd just lean and take the strain. Some of them would just refuse to move a load. You knew they could but they would just play you up.

Carts were well maintained and never left out at night. You would take the wheels off once every fortnight and grease them so they pulled easily. You made the horses' life easy. Carts were all made from wood apart from the metal rim round the wheels and where you hooked the harness on.

Work on the farm was more of a communal thing than it is today. I have now worked on my own for nearly 20 years. When I first started there were eight horses and 11 men on 220 acres. When Mr Sutton sold out I was virtually alone on 300 acres. That will show you how mechanisation has changed.

Of the 11 men two of them would be team men to look after the horses. In winter time there were three bullock feeders and that is a full time job. There were two tractor drivers and the rest were just general labourers.

Some of the hedges you would pile the trimmings up and they would then be used to thatch the hay for the horses to stop the water going in.

I did just about learn to thatch and to horse plough but I was really at the end of it.

There was one pond or pit in the farmyard. When the horses came home after a day's work they would go down into what we called the pit to drink. There was one further down the road which we called the Willow Pit that would be the supply of water for the cattle in winter time.

You would have to cart that with a horse and water cart to the cattle which were kept in sheds and in the yards. I suppose they put tap water in four or five years after I had started but until then it was all done by pail.

I can well remember, in the winter time, you had to fill this water cart with a bucket. You'd back the cart down into the pit, so the horse was ready to pull it out, and you'd fill it with a bucket. The frost sometimes would be that bad you would have a pulp sack round you and the icicles would hang off it. If you didn't stand on the front of the water cart, when it came out of the pit, just before it got to the top it would shoot up and you'd lose the lot. Looking back it was all good fun really!

Late nights

Myrus Sutton, who I worked for, he would go to Ireland, buy a lot of Hereford cattle and bring them back. They would arrive in Thorpe station in cattle trucks. I've been up there at 12 o'clock at night sorting them out and taking them on to various farms by lorry.

Pay

When I first started in 1959 as a boy at 15 the pay was £4.2s.6d. a week. Compared with an apprenticed engineer or carpenter they would only have about 30s. a week.

Accommodation

Nearly everybody on the farm got accommodation; a tied house. The rent was 11s. a week up to 1964 or '65 and that never did go up. So although the pay was low you had a house for a low rent. There was plenty of wood on the farm for your fire.

Work clothes

We wore Army or Airforce coats in winter time, rubber boots and good leather boots. They used to wear the leather buskins up the legs, specially the team men.

Leather buskins were worn to protect the legs, c.1910.

They were like Army gaiters but coming right up to the knee. Good leather boots which you kept well oiled so you never got wet feet. You always had a hat on and woollen gloves or wore a sock on your hands. To protect you when you were topping and tailing sugar beet you would have a pulp sack round you to keep the mud off you.

These are some of Sutton's field names; Rope's Piece, Tuck's piece, Ashen Row, The Grove and Church Piece.

You cut a hedge with a hook and shears. Sometimes you started on a hedge with a pair of shears and it stretched from here to kingdom come! Mainly you used a hedging hook but round the farm it was shears to look tidy.

It was natural fitness, you didn't need a gym.

Michael Mack's family tree goes back to 1641. William Mack moved to Witton Hall in 1890 and Michael's grandfather bought Witton and Home Farm, Blofield, in 1950.

Later his father John farmed at Blofield and uncle Tom Mack at Witton.

Their workers included Billy Parker (foreman), Ray Long, Alec Barber, Tom Rose, Fred Norgate, Bob Goffin and later Donald Chipperfield and his wife, Vera, Wilfred Cator, Arthur Harvey and Cecil Parker.

Arable farming at Home Farm was originally sugar beet, wheat and barley, with broccoli, peas and beans introduced in the early 1990s. Now land is rented out for growing potatoes and lettuces. Irrigation is all important; you provide the water and the ploughed field.

The Mack family, Christmas 1900. Left to right, back row: *Thomas Edward, Ellen Mary, William Richard, Bessie, Edie, Nelson, Kate, Edward*; front row: *Deborah, Helen (child), Elizabeth, Phyllis (child), Edith Hayward, Edmund Hylton (child), John Hayward, John Hayward (child).*

John Mack, late 1980s.

The fields all had names – there was 'Ashyard', 'Park' and 'Bells', where you could hear the bells from the Hall. 'Lord's Piece' was changed to 'West Toft' – perhaps the men didn't like referring to the Lord!

There was a big beech hedge around the lake and an avenue right up through the woods back to Blofield Hall. In the days when Major Harker had the estate the Italian POWs used to cut the hedge with shears; they were the last to cut it and now it is 50 feet high.

Except for his National Service years, **John Oakley** has farmed all his working life with the Mack family at Witton and Blofield, working for three generations – William, John and Michael.

When John was a schoolboy there was a dairy herd at the Blofield farm and he would go after school to get an enamel can of milk straight from the cows and cut across the fields home.

During the war, when he was ten or 11, he was able to take half-days off school to go and help on the farms at such busy times as harvest and haymaking:

You had a green card from the ministry which let you

Cecil Parker. He and Fred were sons of William Parker the foreman.

have 20 half days off school so you could go fruit picking and help out. They would tick your card. We were needed because most of the labour was called up and gone to the war then.

Wartime brought double summer time and work could go on until ten at night during harvest.

I loved the old horses. There used to be about ten on the farm, about the same number of men, I suppose. Horses when they were hot and sweaty would roll in the drinking pit with their saddles on if you didn't look out.

In those days there were pigs, chickens, cattle and the horses. John started work when he left school in 1949:

Men were on £4.10s. a week and I got £1.17s.6d. for a 48 hour week.

We weren't allowed to work on Sundays then. Apart from feeding the horses and milking the cows we never dreamed of doing anything else on a Sunday.

Threshing the stacks
All the corn was cut with sail rigged binders then and was stacked to be threshed out in the winter time. Mr Spanton, who lived opposite the school, had the steam engine and threshing tackle and used to come round the farms.

Arthur Jermy describes:

The whole tackle consisted of the steam engine, the drum in to which the sheaves of corn were fed and

WEEKLY LABOUR ACCOUNT							
	S at	M	T	W	T	F	
WORKMEN'S NAMES	FIRST DAY	SECOND DAY	THIRD DAY	FOURTH DAY	FIFTH DAY	SIXTH DAY	SEVENTH DAY
W Parker	Carting Kale	Carting Sugar	Beet				
B Howard	Hay	Ploughing	Cart; Sugar Beet	Sprd Muck			
C Parker	Pulling	Topping	Sugar Beet	½ Cart yard			
J Lynn	Pulling	S Beet	Spreading	Muck	Park		
F Norgate	Pulling	S Beet	Topping	½ Spread Muck			
F Crisp	Pulling	Sugar	Beet	Topping	Spr Muck		
D Chipperfield	milking	and	yard	work			
F Parker	milking	and	yard	work			
				Oct 22 1948			
W Parker	Carting	Sugar Beet	Clearing up Straw				
C Parker	Tops	Pulling	Carting	Sugar B	Plough		
F Norgate	Spreding	Sugar	Spread;	Carting	TractorHedge		
A Barber	Muck	Beet	Muck	SBet	Carting		
F Parker	Straw	Cart;	SBeet	Carting	Triming		
D Chipperfield	milking	and	yard	work			

Harvest and hospital blues, Home Farm, c.1945.

Cows off Home Field, 1981.

threshed, and the elevator or straw pitcher, as it was commonly called, which carried the straw up to the stack. The threshing operation took several workmen, typically the engine driver, the feeder, who fed the sheaves in to the drum, a bond cutter, who cut the string bonds round the sheaves and the bagman, who attended to the bagging of the grain from the drum. Two or three were pitching the sheaves from the corn stack onto the drum, two or three on the straw stack and the man who tended the chaff bags and cleared the waste.

John Oakley continues:

There would be 12 to 14 stacks in the stack yard after harvest.

When the farmer wanted some money he'd thresh a couple of stacks out. You got about 120 sacks to a stack. The sacks were stacked in the corn barn. On Saturday morning at the corn exchange he took a sample with him to see who'd give him the most for it. A merchant would come and collect the sacks. That was the farmer's living; it paid the wages and let him buy things for the farm.

In the late 1950s combines started coming in. We first hired one from Mr Brewster, who was at Manor Farm.

Flax was being grown for the Ministry to be used for linen and rope and for parachute cords during the war. Flax had to be pulled, you didn't cut it. Just after the war German prisoners did that job.

At Brundall there was a POW camp for the Italians. They used to help with potato picking. They wore brown overalls with a yellow or orange ring on the back and a soldier with a rifle stood there all day watching them. Not that they'd run away. They were on to a good thing; it was better than fighting.

Blofield Hall was a convalescent home for wounded troops during the war. They used to walk about in a blue uniform with a red tie so you knew who they were. They used to come and help with picking up potatoes and trimming hedges.

Old Mr Mack rode a pony. He used to come round every day. Unofficially, he wouldn't allow a breakfast break but we had a bag on our back. We were always on the lookout for Mr Mack coming round on his pony. Somehow or other, though, he always contrived to come a different way from where you were looking. He'd catch you every time. He never said anything, though, he was a very fair boss.

Mr Chipperfield was head cowman and Billy Parker was the foreman. Labour came back and forth at busy times like harvest. Sugar beet was chopped out by hand in those days, pulled up by hand and the tops cut off. A chap who worked there said, 'There's one thing I know. They will never get a machine that'll pull and top beet. We'll never lose that job.' He should be alive today to see them being taken up six rows at a time!

111

Grandfather Spanton's car, 1936. John is inside, Fred and Allen on the running-board and mother and father are in the dickey seat which, Phyllis Jermy remembers, 'opened up like a little bread bin'.

Spanton's sawmill, c.1915, with Frederick Spanton.

In 1951 John Mack started a herd of Friesians. He bought some good cows and went to shows, Peterborough and Aylsham, winning championships. We had turkeys, then pigs. Combines and bailers came in and threshing went out.

A machine came which threshed the peas out in the field. You got them into your lorry and had to be at Yarmouth within 90 minutes of them being shelled out. The advertisement was 'Fresh as the moment the pod went pop.'

If you were late they rejected you. On a Saturday morning on the Acle New road you quite often didn't have a hope of getting them there.

I remember the bad winter of 1962/63 when it froze non-stop for over 100 days. The temperature never got above freezing. That was a year we never finished the sugar beet. It froze into the ground. Cantley factory had to shut up because they weren't getting any beet in. It was left and ploughed in.

John Houghton recalls that his grandfather, Mr Spanton, came from Cottenham Farm at Panxworth to set up his contracting threshing business opposite Blofield School. The family lived in Flora House with an orchard on two acres of land where Manor Ridge stands now. Down Plantation Road, beyond the old school playing-field, stood large sheds which housed the two steam engines, the drum and the elevator. During the winter timber was cut there with a saw bench.

David Morton at Blofield Lodge had cattle and arable land.

Spanton's threshing, c.1915. Jimmy Francis: 'We had eight, ten or sometimes 12 stacks to do and each stack would be a day's threshing. You'd get about 100 comb of corn a day. That was a hard day's work.' In front of the threshing engine is Frederick Spanton.

A bill from F.B. Spanton, 1932.

Manor Farm harvest, 1920s. Harry Edrich is in the invalid chair, Edwin is on the binder and Charlie is immediately to the left of him.

10 pole. (One acre equals 4 roods and one rood is 40 square poles.)

Olive Conlin remembers:

The little dairy was joined to the house and in front was a big pond. They used to make all their own butter and cheeses. Mrs Edrich did all that and my dad used to separate the milk.

Harry Edrich at Manor Farm brought up a family who could field an entire cricket team. In Harry's time Manor Farm encompassed 181 acres 3 rood and

Harry was crippled and in an invalid chair. Charlie went to France in the First World War as a farrier.

The Edrich family, 1920s. Left to right, back row: Harry junr, May, Edwin, George, Fred, John, Harriet, Arthur; middle row: Bill, Elizabeth, Harry senr, Ina, Charlie; seated at front: Alice and Bob.

Threshing at Manor Farm with a 4hp Garrett engine, c.1935. The picture includes: *Charlie Edrich, George Tungate, Arthur Edrich, Billy Butt, Ben Hanton, Walter Knights, Ted Tungate, John Edrich, Billy Frost, Frank Symonds, Herbert Hanton and Spot the dog.*

Harry's sons, John and Edwin, went to farm in Danesbower Lane, where the farm workers were Lenny Hayton and Ted Frost, who worked with the horses. The threshing was done across the road from the farm.

Billy Butt had a donkey and cart and followed the threshing. He was called the 'chaff and colder' man, as he had the dirty job of bagging and clearing the chaff and the muck which came out at the back end of the threshing machine.

Edriches also farmed down Lingwood Road at Garden Farm where, in more recent years, Mr Andrews developed a farm shop with 'pick your own' fruit and vegetables.

Manor Farm was bought, after Harry Edrich's death, by Mr Brewster. As a director of Case & Stewart, a fertiliser factory in Yarmouth, he ran an experimental farm growing on small plots using different fertilisers.

In the October 1944 edition of the deanery magazine was reported a: 'Ploughing Match and Harvest Home in Mr Brewster's field…'

Mr Brewster had bungalows built for his head pigman, farm foreman and other workers beside

Jimmy Hilton feeding mangolds to cattle, Manor Farm, c.1910.

Potato picking ladies, 1960s. Left to right, back row: *Mrs Olive Allen, Mrs Trett, Mrs Bowring, Frank Rope, Mrs Baynes, Mrs Green, Mrs Lockwood, Mrs Rose, Mrs Hayton, Mrs Skedge;* sitting: *Mrs Olive Conlin and Mrs Buxton.*

Before the horse was ousted by the tractor, Heath Farm, October 1964. Left to right: *Percy Buxton on tractor, Polly Green, three boys from Little Plumstead hospital, Ray Thomas leading Boxer and Fred Hubbard leading Queenie.*

Keys' garage on Yarmouth Road, 1964 (opposite Garden Farm).

what was Underdown's garage. More accommodation, the front crescent of Brewster Court, was erected for his retired staff.

Casual Work on the Land

Colin Debbage's story of potato picking as a boy:

The tractor went up and down the field flailing the potatoes out of the ground. We went along picking them up. There were marker sticks so you knew your area where you had to collect all the potatoes but the women used to move the sticks. You'd be working away with your head down and when you looked up you still had ever so much to do. Maybe you were supposed to do 10 yards but you ended up with 20 or 30 yards. Of course the women had all finished!

Keys were motor and agricultural engineers in Blofield and at Norwich cattle market.

Women undertook seasonal work and often worked extremely hard. Lily Barnes, during the war, single-handedly harvested 17 acres of sugar beet each year at Bonds Farm.

Elizabeth Balkwill's drawings of Sam and John Buckland.

Joe Stout and Abiathar Jermy

CHAPTER 8

People from the Past

Miss Lily Ainsworth

Fondly remembered by many as a midwife and as someone who loved people, Lily belonged to virtually all the village organisations, the Girls' Friendly Society being just one of those for which she is remembered. Living a busy life, with her mother and father to care for over many years, she still was never too busy to answer a call for help.

'A really true Christian, she set us an example by her selfless devotion to the community,' stated the parish newsletter, *Blofield News*.

She taught music in Blofield School, was church organist from the 1930s to the 1960s and choir mistress for nearly 36 years, as well as being an able and enthusiastic conductor of the Brundall orchestra.

Josiah Brewster

When Josiah Brewster died in 1972, it was said of him that:

... his sympathies were with those of reduced circumstances and the lovely bungalows which graced the entrance to Blofield were a proof of his generous spirit. Seeking no publicity, the help he gave to so many was always anonymous. The beautiful church lych gate was given in memory of his wife Mary.

He established Brewster Court in 1952 as housing for

Miss Ainsworth, organist until 1962.

his retired employees and stipulated that food parcels and other gifts be delivered to them regularly.

Part of the village scene were the four **Buckland** brothers. Dennis (Tich) and George worked for the Ropes at Street Farm, while Sam and John worked for Did Basey Fisher.

Other familiar faces belonged to **Abiathar Jermy**, who worked for the Ropes, and **Joe Stout**, who was gardener for the Mackintosh family at the Manor House. Their friend, **Lenny Hayton**, is also fondly remembered.

William Codling

In 1845 William Codling, the parish clerk, was a man of considerable position in the parish. As well as being master at Reve's school in Beech House, Clerk to the Magisterial Petty Sessions held at Blofield, Clerk to the Guardians of the Blofield Union (responsible for the Workhouse at Lingwood) and Superintendent of Births and Deaths, he often acted as Will Maker and adviser to other, less literate, parishioners.

In 1820 he planted the line of lime trees bordering the churchyard.

Tom Copeman

Tom Copeman spent long summer holidays at the Mill House in Blofield. His father cherished a belief that country air made children strong. Tom wrote in 1974:

Every spring from 1902 to 1909 a horse-drawn van from a warehouse pulled up outside our house in Norwich to be loaded with beds and bedding, household equipment and even furniture. When all was ready my brother Will and I climbed up beside the driver.

We were bound for Blofield to spend five or six months in the old Mill House, which my father had rented. We savoured the long journey and got down and walked up the hill at Witton Run.

The blue-tiled Mill House was a splendid place for children, even if one year the well ran dry so that we had to rely on minerals and milk. Our outbuildings included a stable for the donkey and a coach house for the chaise in which we drove along roads still innocent of cars.

A large thatched cart shed made a perfect playroom with a sturdy swing.

Sometimes Mr Henry Edrich, our landlord's father, would sit in the sun and watch our play. In the yard we would bowl hoops or whip tops according to the season, while the paddock became a place for kite flying and elementary cricket.

Our walks into the village were enlivened by the glare of the blacksmith's forge and the music of his hammer. On the turnpike a wheelwright named Key had a thriving business.

Many of the old ways were slowly dying. The courteous 'I bid you good morning' was to have its first three words clipped off and the old plural forms 'housen' and 'childer' would soon be heard no more. When did the musical 'Aaklee' become the prosaic Acle?

Our neighbours were two unmarried brothers, Elijah and Elisha Key, whose sister Charlotte kept house for them. They had a dairy herd and we were allowed glimpses of milking, separating or churning and, once every summer, watched the brewing of the harvest beer.

This delightful and welcoming family soon made us free of their harvest fields where, as we grew older, Will and I were able to give a hand, as most boys loved to do. The farm was small and except at harvest, I fancy, only one outside man, old Manthorpe, was employed. Elijah, however, was moving with the times and was especially proud of his self-binder.

A neighbouring and bigger farmer still used an old-fashioned affair with 'sails' which meant that the corn had to be picked up and tied into sheaves by hand. If a field was badly laid it had to be cut by scythe and I remember seeing the line of mowers being followed by another line of women who used wisps of straw for binding.

For us the great moment came when the self-binder was nearing the end of its task on the Key's field by the Turnpike. Only a small square of corn remained uncut, but how many rabbits did it hold? A small group of villagers began to gather as Elisha got his gun ready, and someone showed me how to kill the rabbit I never caught. Suddenly there were excited shouts as the poor creatures dashed out, to become welcome additions to more than one supper.

I always loved that outlying field because often it meant a ride to the stack yard on the top of a load. Before that happened the field would be a beautiful sight with neat lines of shocks. Within a few days they would be lifted amid cries of 'hold ye' to make a neat stack near the farmhouse. One final rite remained. The ancient custom of gleaning still lingered as a privilege of women and children. Sheets and bags could hold a lot if a farmer was sparing with his rake; and there was still one windmill not far off.

I remember a strange incident at the end of one harvest. Old Manthorpe unexpectedly appeared at the Mill House, a picturesque figure with his smock and fringe of beard. In a quavering voice he began to cry 'largess' to my surprised and puzzled parents.

Only years later did I realise that I had heard the last dying echo of a custom which had come down from the Middle Ages. The words were 'halloo largess,' a corruption of 'à la largess' and should properly be shouted thrice after the reapers had received a gift.

Miss Cubitt worked for 45 'tireless' years for the Red Cross. Here she is receiving her British Empire Medal from the Lord Lieutenant of Norfolk, Sir Edmund Bacon, in the Margaret Harker Hall in 1973.

Labourers' wages were low and it was an accepted custom to visit the more well-to-do members of the parish to beg for 'largesse'. This practice gave way to the custom, renewed in churches in recent years, of a supper to celebrate the safe bringing in of the harvest.

Miss Olive Cubitt

Olive Cubitt had a long and energetic association with the Red Cross, which she joined in 1928, holding the post of commandant for 26 years until 1972.

As salvage steward during the war she was in charge of the collection of aluminium, paper, etc., and during the East Coast floods of 1953 she worked to bring relief to stricken families.

Her voluntary duties at Little Plumstead hospital are remembered as 'outstanding work'. Along with Miss Ainsworth, she led the Girls' Friendly Society.

Sir Peter Eade, 1825–1915

Growing up in Blofield, Peter enjoyed cricket, boating and fishing. The family owned land which was intensively cultivated, not with conventional crops but with such things as white poppies, henbane and roses. From the poppies, with careful preparation, came the wonder drug of the age, *Extractum papaveris*.

His father, Dr Eade, practised surgery and medicine in Blofield for 35 years from 1825. He apprenticed the young Peter who, during five years of training, learned about drugs, dispensing, book-keeping and even performed some minor surgery.

After more training in London he returned with a doctorate in medicine and took up work with his father.

Peter Eade as a young man.

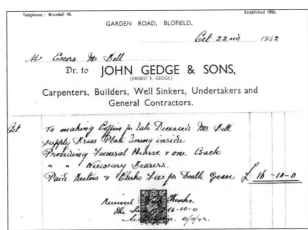

A bill from Gedge & Sons.

In 1856 he moved to Norwich and began a brilliant career as physician at the Norfolk and Norwich hospital; he had work published in *The Lancet* and became a member of the Royal College of Physicians. Living in a large house in Upper Giles Street, he gained a number of eminent appointments in medicine.

During three terms of office as mayor of the city he instigated the provision of public parks and open spaces, and was congratulated for 'his anxious efforts to give us wider breathing spaces and to lighten our dull rows of streets with spots of natural beauty.'

Appointed magistrate at the age of 46, he remained one for 41 years!

Blofield School benefited from his generosity and his desire to provide activity in the open air when he proposed giving a piece of land adjoining the site to be used by the children for school gardening. This he proceeded to rent for the school from Mr Redgment, the landowner.

On his death in 1915 he was buried in Blofield churchyard. The east window of the church is given in memory of him.

The Gedge Family

The business of John Gedge & Son was formed in Blofield in 1866. The family had lived at Tresco on the Yarmouth Road but later at their house in Garden Road with a paddock behind for their horses.

A builder in a village had wood to make coffins and a horse and cart to take the coffin to church. One firm of builders and funeral directors had the saying 'if we don't build your house we will bury you.'

Stanley Gedge joined the building trade at 14, learning many skills, including that of digging wells.

In his later years, he said, he could walk about the village and pick out the many houses he had built. He was optimistic for the future of his family firm, now run by Chris Gedge and his wife Sue.

Roy Granger, 1908–2001

Roy Granger came to the village in 1946, served on the Parochial Church Council for 50 years and was president of the Norfolk Archaeological Society. 'I've always been interested in history,' he said.

Many people in the parish learned a great deal from Roy on any historical subject they asked him about; he brought history to life for young and old, each time he spoke.

Roy Granger (right) *in June 1996 with Archdeacon Handley on Roy's retirement after 50 years' service with the Parochial Church Council.*

William Lightfoot Hague, school attendance officer, with his wife and children at Wakefield Villa, Garden Road, 1910. Left to right, back row: *Flo, Syd, Doris;* middle row: *Pat on the lap of William, Edith with Cassie (later Turner);* front row: *Cyril, Tip (the dog), Reggie.*

Cyril Hague

In 1970 the *Blofield News* reported:

Cyril Hague was a member of a well known and respected Blofield family. He was one of the original Blofield troop of Boy Scouts before the 1914 war, and when the Recreation Ground was provided as a war memorial, he organised the Bowls Club. He served as its Honorary Secretary and became Singles Bowls Champion of Norfolk County. For many years he shared in our worship at Blofield Church as a fine tenor singer in that Choir which, under the late Canon Shillito, was so highly esteemed in this Diocese.

Margaret Harker, 1880–1935

As well as being deeply involved in her local Red Cross work, Margaret Harker served as a Justice of the Peace and was a regular worshipper at Blofield Parish Church.

A Scot herself, she felt an empathy with the Scottish fisher girls who followed the herring fleets to Great Yarmouth. These 'girls', some 16, some in their 60s, sustained many injuries gutting herring. Working at lightning speed with sharp knives, their hands were often cut and ulcerated by contact with salt.

Margaret set up a Red Cross dressing station in

Yarmouth and in just one season of seven and a half weeks, nearly 7,000 dressings were applied. She was fond of this aspect of her work and would spend much time with the girls and join in their songs.

She and her husband gave the parish its hall which, after her death, was renamed the Margaret Harker Hall.

Dr John McKelvie

Older residents remember Dr McKelvie, a real character who was sometimes outspoken. But, as Olive Conlin comments:

Dr McKelvie was so kind. It would be nothing for him to go into the butcher's shop to take six pennyworth of sausages to someone's house, without anyone knowing, because he'd know it was really needed.

He enjoyed tennis and bowls: 'You always knew where to find the doctor… at the bowling green.'

Rose Bates, midwife, lived with her family at Minns Farm and Dr McKelvie would call for her in his car, a Standard, and take her out on cases. During the day she would cycle to her patients to do follow-up visits.

Dr McKelvie's successor, Dr Evans, was sometimes called out to a case at Surlingham. He would drive down to the river to be ferried across, at times by Ted Ellis the naturalist, and was collected by car on the other side to be taken to the patient's home.

Hilda Rope

Mrs Hilda Rope was a much loved infant teacher at Blofield School. When she retired in 1951, after 32 years, she was presented with a leather handbag from the children and a cheque from the parents.

However she was soon called back on 'temporary duty' for two terms which grew to be at least five years. At one stage, with the school bursting at the seams, she taught an extra class in the woodwork room and Mrs Turner's class had to meet in the committee room at the Margaret Harker Hall.

Finally, in about 1956, Mrs Rope was allowed to retire.

The Royals at Beech House

When the two board schools were built, Beech House was no longer needed as a school and the Royal family later bought it from the Reve Trust.

Mrs Shirley Royal writes: 'In the 1930s Susannah Royal had a succession of village boys who ran errands for her up the alley to the shops. She called them her "grooms".'

When she died the village lost a link with the Victorian age.

Her daughter, Evelyn (Eva) Royal, was a kindly

The Royal family in Beech House garden, 1925. Left to right, standing: *Eva, Albert Harry (her brother);* front, sitting: *Susannah with John on her lap, Albert's wife, Hilda, with Mary and baby Michael.*

teacher at Strumpshaw School and a Sunday-school teacher in Blofield Church. She served the church for many years and was involved in many village organisations. She died in 1975 at the age of 95.

In her ninety-third year she wrote that, as a three-year-old, she sat on the lap of her great-great uncle, Joseph Bane, and, in a quavering voice, he sang to her the old song 'The Death of Nelson'. He could distinctly remember the Battle of Trafalgar and the mourning on Nelson's death, although he had only been a small child at the time.

Joseph was a kind hearted man. From the school log-book:

Mr Joseph Bane, the oldest inhabitant of Blofield, provided 20 whips for 20 of the best fellows in the infant room. He liked to make whips, reins etc during his leisure time and distribute them to the youngsters.

His father, Matthew Bane, had helped ring the Victory Peals for both Trafalgar and Waterloo.

In 1968 Eva wrote:

About the year 1800, the Griffin Inn, on the corner of the Street and Doctors Road, was kept by Matthew Bane, born 1770. He was my great-great-grandfather. I have his large and well thumbed prayer book, dated 1770.

Matthew's daughter, Sarah, married William

Stockens, born 1799, who built the present Rectory (in Stocks Lane) and several other houses in Blofield.

The Stockens family has been traced back to c.1680. At some point they changed their name to Stockings but the original name may be derived from Flemish weavers who settled in East Anglia.

Before Matthew Bane kept the Inn I think it was kept by Thomas Emerson, 1720–1802. He was my great-great-great grandfather and is buried near the old church gate.

Mrs Doris Mayes remembers that Miss Royal commemorated Trafalgar Day each 21 October by covering with a union flag a box which had come from one of the ships of the fleet.

Obadiah Smith

When Obadiah Smith, Blofield's postmaster of 32 years, died in 1970, Mr Bates, a later postmaster, wrote:

Blofield has lost a true and great friend. He served in the Army during the First World War with distinction and was decorated by the late king George V, who said to him 'I see you come from Norfolk – I too have a home there.'

During the Second World War he was involved with many activities which were necessary to the well-being of village life under difficult conditions.

Fred Starling, 1865–1957

Fred Starling was a pupil at the Reve school, where his father William taught.

He was chosen for the church choir at the age of six but was trained for two years before he was allowed to join. While he was a choirboy the incumbent was the Revd Turnbull, who dispensed stockings to the boys and flannel for petticoats to the girls.

Fred recalled that the needy of the parish, coming each week to the rector for help, were rarely disappointed. He helped the rector hand out loaves of bread after the service on a Sunday until 'The people got so independent and proud they would not take them.'

Fred found a coffin cage in about 1941 in some laurel bushes in the churchyard. At one time relatives would pay men to watch a grave for three nights or have the grave covered by a cage. This would have a metal grid held down by four spikes and made exhumation so difficult that no body snatcher would attempt it.

The cage he found was destined for the British Museum but initially went to the blacksmith, as it was slightly damaged. The blacksmith cleaned it up and tarred it but the museum then turned it down as it was not in its original condition. Fred was very

The team of handbell ringers outside Blofield School, c.1910. Left to right: Randall Ward (junr), ? Gedge, Walter Read (the tailor), ?, Herbert Trett, Fred Starling, Randall Ward (senr). In 1934 it was reported that 'this was the fifty-fourth year Mr F. Starling had been round the parish with handbells on Boxing Day.'

Hardley Symonds, village shoemaker.

annoyed when, stored away in the rectory loft, it eventually went missing. Possibly it was given away during the war as scrap metal!

Fred's grandfather had helped to build the new piece of road from the King's Head to the corner of Doctors Road in about 1810.

In his later years Fred visited Dr McKelvie, feeling unwell. 'My boy,' said the doctor, 'go to the King's Head every morning and have a glass of Guinness and you will feel better.' 'And so I am!' Fred recounted later.

To commemorate his years as a bell-ringer he was presented with a wallet inscribed '1873–1953'.

When he retired from the choir, after 80 years, some members wanted to give him a book, to which he replied that he had one. To the suggestion of a chair came the same answer. When offered a watch he replied, 'You know at my time of life you don't care much about the time as long as it keeps going.'

The money which had been collected was lodged at the King's Head so that he could continue his daily visits and this he did until he left Blofield to stay with his daughters.

Hardley Symonds

Valerie Howes, niece of Hardley Symonds, writes of the war years she spent at Blofield Heath.

Born in 1940, Valerie spent most of the first five years of her life living at Blofield Heath with her uncle and aunt, Mr and Mrs Hardley Symonds. Her mother was with her but her father was away in Coventry working in munitions.

My uncle was named after the village of Hardley, south of Norwich, where he was born. Hardley was the village cobbler and knew and was known by most people in the area and was always ready for a 'mardle'. He was kept extremely busy when sack loads of boots and shoes arrived from Little Plumstead hospital to be repaired.

He made me summer sandals and I was the envy of all my friends as they were definitely originals. His workshop was great fun for me and I would try on as many pretty pairs of shoes as I could before they were repaired.

Looking back it seems to me there was a great village spirit with everybody knowing each other. Hardley would go off and do his share of Home Guard duties. My aunt only had a small oven in the wall but produced delicious meals. There was no running water, a pail toilet down the garden and a copper in the shed where Aunt had a boil up once a week.

Next door to the workshop was the chapel and music drifted over in summer evenings when doors and windows were open. Long summer days, never mind there being a war on, I was very happy and had lots of lovely things to do. Happy days for a small child being indulged in a very simple way.

Hardley died in 1969 and Aunt Doris a few years later.

CHAPTER 9

Sports and Groups

Sport at Blofield's Recreation Ground

By 1926 the tennis, bowls and cricket clubs at the hall were all flourishing:

There are four excellent tennis courts. The annual subscription is 10 shillings. The Bowls club has one of the best greens in the County and membership is open to all who pay a subscription of 5 shillings a year. Cricketers – an interesting list of fixtures has been made and there is a useful wicket for net practice always available. Cricketers in the district are invited to join at once. The subscription is 5 shillings and the Hon. Sec. is Mr Edwin Edrich.

In the 1950s it was said that: 'Blofield is fortunate in possessing recreation grounds at the Heath and near the church. These are venues for football and cricket matches, fêtes, shows etc.'

The Football Club
by Barry Murphy

Blofield has supported a football club from the early twentieth century up to the present with barely a break. Early records show a team playing in the East Norfolk Village League. During that era the home ground was called Chamberlin's Park or Callow Green. Some recall visiting teams being collected from Brundall railway station by horse and cart.

In 1923 the club began playing at Blofield recreation ground for the first time. By 1936 records show the club playing in the Norwich and District league, the secretary was H. White and the colours were green and amber. Blofield Heath also formed a team in 1928, their secretary was R. Webb and colours were blue and amber.

Blofield withdrew from the league and disbanded in 1960 but several members joined with a team of youngsters playing as Brundall Minors (since 1959). They rejoined the league as Brundall United in 1961 and play resumed on Blofield Rec. Quickly moving through the Norwich and District league divisions, they became champions in 1966 and then moved to join the Anglian Combination as members of division four.

Rapid progress was made; within three seasons the team was in division two and by 1972 had

Blofield Football Club, 1937. Left to right, back row: ? Nicholls (referee), George Nicholls, 'Knock' Cutler, Bobby Key, Verdun Willgress, Freddy Stone, Billy Futter, Herbert White, front row: Ted Drinkwater, Jack Mingay, Frank 'Muggy' Read, Leonard Layt, Alan Weston, Jack Long, Edwin Edrich (linesman). By the pavilion are Walter Horner and Cecil Baynes.

Blofield Heath football team, 1945. Left to right, back row: *Cecil Howes (trainer), Freddy Tubby, George (Boo) Nichols, Frank Atkins, Tim Nicholls, Leslie Basey-Fisher, Eric Martin (manager);* front row: *Gerald Stapleton, Bryan Grapes, ?, Tom Nicholls, Roger Jermy, Noel King, Sid Barrett.*

Blofield football team, 1963. Left to right, back row: *Evan Gitsham, Freddie Pluckrose, Pat Clarke, Peter Mayes, Freddie Colk, Pip Tallents;* front row: *Eddie Willimott, Paddy Murphy, Peter Griffiths, Clive Griffiths, Simon Nobbs, John High.*

finally in 1990 a new clubroom replaced the wooden pavilion.

The following season Blofield, as the club had renamed itself in 1992, won the premier division and with it the Sterry Cup. After winning the senior knockout cup in 1993 Blofield were Sterry Cup champions again in 1994. After three Norfolk senior cup semi-final defeats between 1994 and 1998, Blofield returned to winning the premier division Sterry Cup in 2001 and, after a few lean seasons, won it again in 2005, when they achieved the distinction of not losing a league fixture all season.

Familiar Blofield names appear on team photographs over the years, such as Edrich, Rope, Gowing and Basey-Fisher, all farming families from the village, whilst some families have represented the club over several generations, for instance three generations of Murphys and four generations of Basey-Fishers.

Cricket

The Edrich family could field a cricket team plus scorer and umpire!

Harry and Elizabeth Edrich had 13 children, nine boys and four girls. All the boys played cricket and one of the girls, Alice, made 100 against Acle. Over the years several Edriches were county players and Bill and John were capped for England.

They played in village teams, also enjoying village football and tennis.

attained senior status. Several more successful seasons followed and in 1977–78 the club became division one champions and moved into the premier division. After two seasons the club was relegated back to division one but soon returned to the premier division in 1984.

Success on the pitch was matched by the successful fund-raising efforts of a large group of members and supporters plus local businesses and

The Edrich family team v. Falcons IX at Bolfield in 1938. Left to right: *George C., George H., Edwin, Arthur, Harry 'Mac', Geoffrey, Brian, Eric, Alan, William A. and William J. Edrich.*

Horace Webb, from Blofield Heath Post Office, was proud that he once bowled out Bill Edrich with his first ball.

Edrich elevens often played against celebrities in Lord's Taverners matches at Ingham, raising much money for the National Playing Fields Association.

Village Cricket Teams
By Monty Elson, October 2005

Cricket at Blofield in the late 1950s and the early 1960s was played for enjoyment. Of course, we always liked to win, and we always played to win, but the priority was to enjoy the game. Because of this we did not play in a league, and we avoided the stress of an over-competitive situation. All our games were 'friendlies'.

This 'fun' element in our game was probably never better illustrated than in a game played on our own pitch at Blofield. We were batting, and I was at the bowler's end when the bowler sent down a rather loose delivery. My fellow batsman hit the ball back over the bowler's head for six, straight over the hedge into a neighbouring garden. Play was suspended while several of the fielders went and searched for the ball. They returned, and the umpire signalled for the bowler to resume his over.

He ran up to bowl again. This time he sent down

The village cricket team, 1938. Left to right, back row: *Ted Drinkwater, Joe Webb, Roger Wade, Tom Carter, Harry Hammond, Edwin Edrich;* middle row: *Frank Futter, Len Underdown, Alan Weston, John Mingay;* front row: *Dougie Rogers, Alan Edrich.*

a full toss, and as I saw the ball in the air I remember thinking that it looked a little out of shape. The batsman at the other end had no such doubts. Seeing the possibility of another six, he struck the ball a mighty blow.

125

The village cricket team in 1959. Left to right, back row: *Herbert White (umpire), Mike Hughes, Grahame Baynes, Harry Hammond, Terry Carter, Monty Ellson;* middle row: *Harry Deasley, Diana Hammond (scorer), Roy Debbage;* front row: *Wilf Graver, Kingsley Lloyd, David Eastwood, Geoffrey Deasley.*

Tennis at Blofield Lodge, early 1950s. Left to right, back row: *Mr New, Harry Meadows, George Basey-Fisher, Charlie Morton, Phil Greenhill;* front row: *Leslie Basey-Fisher, Gerald Basey-Fisher, George (Did) Basey-Fisher, David Morton.*

Members of the tennis club with a seat in memory of George ('Did') Basey-Fisher, 2000. Seated are Babs and Barbara, his widow and daughter.

The ball completely disintegrated, and the batsman, several fielders in front of the bat, and myself at the other end were spattered with purple juice.

As well as finding the ball in the garden, the bowler had picked up a beetroot, and it was that which he lobbed down so invitingly. It wasn't until we stopped laughing that we began to realise how difficult a job it was going to be for our ladies to turn us out in unspotted whites for the next match.

Tennis
by Glenna Butler and Liz Waller

Blofield Tennis Club was formed in 1924 and is probably one of the oldest tennis clubs in Norfolk.

Whereas only private houses and farm gardens had previously had tennis courts, now club tennis could be enjoyed and Mr and Mrs Lincoln and their son Dick were early pioneers. The names Barrett, Edrich, Hammond, Helsdon, Key, Rope and Wadge were among the pre-war players.

Mixed doubles afternoons were social occasions with tea taken in the hall pavilion, although the rivalry on court was far from social.

Affiliation to the Lawn Tennis Association in 1948 allowed Glenna Rope and Gerald Basey-Fisher to play in the Norfolk Junior Championships and most years since then have seen Blofield juniors participate in county events.

Membership now is open to all ages and standards, with 46 adult and 37 junior members. A traditional new pavilion with changing facilities was opened in 1997. Weekly club nights and frequent club tournaments are held throughout the summer months, our teams competing in the Norwich District Jewson Mixed League, having reached division 2, and the Ladies' City League, division 1.

Blofield Badminton Club
by Petra Searle, Ann Hutchin and Graham Cooper

Blofield Badminton Club was formed in 1933 and the following year won its first competitive match against a team from Reedham. Playing in the Margaret Harker Hall, some early members were Peter Tacon and Dick Burton, who gave the Burton Cup for an annual mixed-doubles tournament.

The senior club plays on two evenings each week through the winter months.

A Saturday evening junior section for 11–18-year-olds began in the 1950s, and in 1968 Petra Searle, with Glenna Butler, started a small group for under 11s, playing earlier in the evening. Those first six 'mini-juniors' were Susan and Linda Butler, Suzanne Clarke, Joanna Searle, Rodney Smithdale and John Allison. The fee then was 2d. per session attended!

In around 1970 the junior section expanded rapidly,

Some members of the badminton club, November 2005. Left to right, back row: *Sandra Robinson, Ann Hutchin, Ian Murphy, Gavin Broad, Yvonne Easton;* front row: *Sarah Lewin, Charlotte Crosby, Lee Robinson, Daniel Leers.*

hiring the Margaret Harker Hall most Saturdays from 9.30 in the morning to 8.30 in the evening, the day being divided into six ability sessions.

The Junior Badminton Club was very popular, having 90–100 children and a waiting list. Groups of boys and girls have become lifelong friends, meeting on a Saturday for their weekly get together.

The Christmas fancy-dress tournament was the social highlight of the year; losers of every game had to don some impediment – wellies, mukluks, tennis racquets and assorted clothes. A lasting memory is of one girl whose feet, in outsize wellies, could not keep up with her body and she eventually fell flat on the floor.

Petra and Bunty Munday worked together coaching juniors. Mary Hall and her daughter, Jeanette Lovatt, in the 1980s and 1990s, were key coaches, along with Ian Murphy and others for the Junior Club. Don Heath was the treasurer for many years.

The club now ranks as one of the leading senior and junior clubs in the county. Initially entering four teams in the league in 1975, the club now has seven teams in the Norwich and District League. In the 2004/05 season Blofield Badminton Club were the champions of Division 1, Mixed Ladies and Men's Leagues.

Many players have gone on to play and represent Norfolk Badminton Association and to be County Champions both at junior and senior level. They include Michael Hall, Lizzie Easton, Linda Butler, Ian Murphy and Katherine Cooper, to name just a few.

In the autumn of 2005 the club pulled off a remarkable triumph by taking all five titles in the 2005 Norfolk Restricted Tournament for seniors, the County Championships, a feat never before achieved and one unlikely to be repeated.

In the early days, as now, Monday and Friday nights are badminton nights but some things have changed. In 1975/76 the hall could be hired for the season for £133 and a dozen shuttles cost £3.

The Winter Walking Group
by Malcolm Bishop

Started in 2000 by Malcolm Bishop, this small informal group walks the local lanes and footpaths on two afternoons each week during the winter months. Our aim is to get some exercise and enjoy the winter scenery and wildlife with like-minded company.

The winter walking group, 2005. Left to right: Barry Wood, Jack Palmer, Fred Stubbs, Marie Palmer, Jim Beebey, Petra Searle, Bob Bulley.

The Blofield and District Conservation Group
by David Pilch

The Blofield and District Conservation Group was founded in 1983 and soon became known by the acronym BADCOG. Its genesis grew out of the concerns of the three founding families, the Hewards, the Pilches and the Roses, that much of our local natural habitat was being lost through neglect, carelessness and ignorance. The catalyst which triggered this concern into action was the sorry state of Holly Lane pond. A local lady, Mrs Irene Faiers, recalled that in the past it had been a picturesque spot full of aquatic plants and animals and, of course, an important watering-place for the working farm horses. In contrast, there was no open water and several felled dead elm trees lay across the pond.

With the aim of the restoration of this pond as a first project, the group was formed. From the outset it was envisaged that the appeal should be to all ages. Thus not only practical work but monthly informative meetings, outings and children's activities such as the popular 'Go Wild Days' would be organised.

The Holly Lane pond restoration was encouraged by the local landowner, John Mack, and was so successful that BADCOG received a Shell Better Britain award for its efforts.

BADCOG has since become involved in a whole range of projects in Blofield and the vicinity. There are work parties every fortnight throughout the year. These have been likened to a 'green gym' and include:
1. Tree planting and hedges – roadside and field, new woodlands in Acle, Blofield, Buckenham, Burlingham, Lingwood, Moulton, and Strumpshaw.
2. Fen and meadow management in Blofield and South Walsham.
3. Churchyard conservation schemes in Blofield, Hemblington, Lingwood, Limpenhoe and Southwood.
4. Pond management at Blofield, Burlingham, Lingwood and Moulton.
5. Woodland management at Buckenham, Mouton, and Strumpshaw.

In addition to managing sites for councils (parochial church, parish, district and county) the group owns two local nature reserves – Railway Wood at Strumpshaw and Jary's Meadow at South Walsham.

BADCOG's enthusiasm and expertise has been recognised over the years by three further Better Britain awards, including best for Anglia in 1989. Its

A BADCOG workparty at Jary's Meadow, December 2005. Left to right: Richard Westgate, Tony Bowyer, John Houghton, David Cullen, Tony Howes, David Payne, Ernest Hoyos, Tony McKie.

Blofield Heath Bowls Club prizegiving, 1981. Left to right: Donald Bunyan, Kay Picton, Kathleen Travis, ?, Olive Henderson, Ray Genery, Bill Henderson, Daisy Perrot, Mary Pointer, Roy Travis.

The Extend group in the Courthouse, 1988. Left to right, back row: *?, ?, Vi Bickers, Pauline Hirst, Joy Foulger, Doreen Green;* middle row: *Jean Rammage;* front row: *Kath Storey, Mary Gentle, Edie Latham, Léa Lazar, ?.*

long-standing chairman and driving force, Ernest Hoyos, received the Norfolk Volunteer of the Year award in 2005. The group looks forward to its silver jubilee in 2008.

Blofield Heath Bowls Club
by Ray Genery

In 1922 the Harker family gave four acres of land to the parish of Blofield for recreational purposes.

In 1926 a group of men from the village formed the framework of the present Bowls Club, laying the green on the present site and carrying out the work needed to make it playable. Mr F. Spanton was elected as chairman, Major Harker was invited to be president and Mr J. Earl was chosen as club captain. They played their first matches in 1926; the first lost against Panxworth, the second, a home match, won easily.

In 1927 the club expanded to 22 playing members and committee members; matches were played as far away as Swardeston.

In 1929 they joined the South Walsham league and grew in quality and strength up to 1938.

Then there seems to have been a lapse in club affairs until 1940 when, after a general meeting, the club restarted. Understandably, it lapsed during the war years, and Major Harker was president when it reformed in November 1948.

At the present time there are about 30 members, with two mixed leagues and one ladies' league all doing well. The club chairman is Mr R. Genery, captain is Mr M. Hollis and president is Mr K. Marshall. The year 2006 is the club's eightieth year.

Blofield, Brundall and District Pensioners' Association
by Joan Williams

This group started up in 1995 when a small number of like-minded pensioners decided to get together, air their views on problems relevant to retired people and try to help.

The first meetings were held monthly in the Margaret Harker Hall and, as the 1997 election approached, interest in the newly formed group grew rapidly. Affiliation with the larger Norfolk Pensioners' Association followed and a written constitution was compiled.

The programme varies between speakers on subjects relevant to the elderly, information on health problems, pensions, tax queries and many other topics. Entertainment is also included.

After the 1997 election membership fell off and it became necessary to move to a smaller venue, the courthouse. Surprisingly, with a slight change to our format, membership started to increase to such an extent that the group now has a waiting list, although visitors are never turned away.

The group goes from strength to strength so we must be doing something right!

Blofield Heath WI
by Marjorie Bloomfield

It was early in 1965 that two members of our community wondered about the possibility of starting a branch of the Women's Institute in our village. Enquiries were made and, following a good response,

Blofield Heath Womens Institute, late 1960s, in the wooden 'hut' before Heathlands Community Centre was built. Left to right, standing: *Val Youngs, Pat Watling, Jean Gulliver, Jean Yaxley, Nancy Jelves, Doris Cox, ?, Daphne Nicholls, Daphne Reeve, Dorothy Hale, Margaret Braithwaite, Phyllis Gilby, Freda Jarvis, Marjorie Englefield, Peggy Foulkes, Jill Senior, Ann Bond, Hilda Nicholls, Sue Hartley;* front, seated: *Marjorie Bloomfield, Sylvia Palgrave-Moore.*

Members of Blofield Women's Institute celebrate its eightieth birthday on 15 January 1998. Mrs Ellen Basey-Fisher, who joined in 1954, was the longest serving member. The photograph includes: Gwenda Gross, Margaret Harding, Betty Thompson, Hilda Gandy, Marie Horne, Nesta Getliffe, Mary Fowler, Edith Latham, Irene Nellor, Louie Smith, Doreen Green, Edna Murch, Ellen Basey-Fisher, Mary Lee, Vi Green, Flo Berry, Elsie Barber, Joy Foulger, Cathy Storey, Pauline Hirst, Barbara Sargant and Doreen Fleury.

Blofield Heath Women's Institute was formed in 1965.

Over the years membership has remained constant and many firm and lasting friendships have been made. Initially, meetings were held in the old wooden hut that served the community at that time. The old hut had 'central heating' in that there was a wood stove in the middle of the floor with a pipe going up through the roof. In winter, when the stove was alight, you couldn't sit too near or you would burn too, but at the sides there were cracks where the walls should have met the floor and the wind whistled through there and chilled you to the bone! A new hall was definitely needed! From the very start we were involved in fund-raising with the 'tote' to build a new Village Hall, which was opened by Lord and Lady Bacon in the early 1970s. After the new buildings at Heathlands were erected, a more pleasant venue was enjoyed by all.

The members of the WI were, and still are, involved in many activities in the community, including getting the village sign, producing the village handbook, starting and continuing to run the day centre for the elderly and needy, and getting daffodils planted on the Blofield and Brundall roundabout to mark the millennium, to name but a few.

We have just celebrated our fortieth birthday with a great celebration, and two of our founder members are still with us.

Blofield WI

The oldest Women's Institute in Norfolk, founded in 1918, held its meetings at the Manor House home of its first president, Mrs Griffiths, an indomitable lady who did much in the village. She was followed by Mrs Harker of Blofield Hall and members met in the Granary in Church Road until the parish hall was opened in 1923.

In the early 1990s its president was Mrs Léa Lazar and there were 32 members. Over the years they have taken part in horticultural shows, pageants and have appeared at the Norfolk show promoting the WI's work. Sadly this branch has now closed.

Blofield Ladies
by Barbara Hardy

Blofield Ladies was formed in 1973 as 'Young Wives' by Gill Dixon, wife of the rector. Meetings were held in the old rectory in Stocks Lane until Nicholas and Gill moved to Cumbria.

As membership changed so did our name. 'Young Wives' became 'Blofield Wives' and then 'Blofield Ladies', in case single ladies felt excluded. As our name changed, so did our venues. Over the years we have met at the school, the courthouse, the Red Cross Hut (now demolished) and in 2006 meet in the Margaret Harker Hall. Our membership has never been very high; at present we have about 36 ladies.

Over the years we have held various fund-raisers for charities – jumble sales, lunches etc. Our main fund-raising event was an annual May Fair which raised, on average, £400– £500 a year. We worked on the basis that our members voted for a project outside the village one year and a local one the next. Our fund raising is not on such a scale now, but we still support various charities, some of which are suggested by the speakers at our monthly meetings.

The Day Centre
by Lynda Beck

Heathlands Day Centre was set up by Ray and Vera Wales and a band of volunteer helpers in 1991. When

An entertainment by some of the helpers at the day centre. Standing at back: *Iris Langford;* left to right, back row: *Pam Flowers, Vera Wales, Ray Wales, Ingrid Newton, Barbara Wheeler, Andrée Raven, Aylis Boon, Norman Faiers;* front row: *Juliet Hague, Gill Ward, Rene Sargant, Rene Faiers, Betty Pugh.*

Enjoying board games at the day centre. The picture includes, from left to right: Ron Bird, Barbara Wheeler, Carol Culham, Bridget Rushbrook, Ivy Ryan, Brenda Unsworth; in the background: Marjorie Bloomfield, Ray Wales, Annie Taylor, Vera Wales.

Ray and Vera retired in April 2004 Lynda Beck stepped into their shoes. Lynda explains:

It is held every Monday at Heathlands Community Centre, the objective being to provide day care for lonely, housebound, isolated, elderly or disabled people. The catchment area is Blofield, Blofield Heath, Hemblington and Pedham.

The centre will accommodate up to 30 people and a hot meal, cooked on the premises, is provided. Various games are played; Scrabble, Upwords, cards, Ludo, dominoes and bingo. Other activities are community singing, musical entertainments and 'Extend', a class in gentle exercise, is held once a month. Annual events are trips on the river, an outing to Yarmouth with a fish and chip lunch, and Christmas and birthday parties.

The Over 60s Club, now named the Over 55s

Mrs Mackintosh, Mrs Henderson-Gray and Miss Cubitt were running the club in the late 1970s when Mrs Hosier took over. Her daughter, Sarah, and then Helen Gallaway and George Catlin have all led the group through the years, with George Hancock the most recent organiser of meetings and outings. Company and entertainment are provided at monthly gatherings and summer coach trips have visited such places as Lincoln, Southwold, Bury St Edmunds, Anglesey Abbey, Windsor and Duxford, to name just a few.

Blofield Pre-School Playgroup
by Louise Guymer

A registered charity run by a voluntary committee of parents and carers, the playgroup opens for four sessions a week in the Margaret Harker Hall, with an attached parent and toddler group meeting on Tuesday afternoons.

On 18 May 1970 the first meeting of Blofield's playgroup was held. Those who set it up included Maria

Members of the Over 55s, 2005. Left to right, back row: Betty Docwra, Flo Berry, Doug Holmes, Mrs Whiffler, Mr Whiffler, June Rogers, Gary Rogers; middle row: Margaret Smart, Dorothy Burdett, Joan Williams, Peggy Robb, Miss Falgate, Eric Newstead, Helen Gallaway, Frank Dunnett; front row: George Hancock, Celia Murphy, Vi Green, Doreen Green, Dot Cooper, Mrs Laws.

Christine Colman with some of her helpers from the play-group planting a flowering cherry tree in June 1976.

Rope, Gill Dixon, Lynne Monck and Gwen Roberts.

Playgroup has changed in some ways since those early days, and is now inspected by the governing body, Ofsted, but ultimately the ethos is the same – for parents and children to meet and learn through play.

We get involved with the local community, organising visits to Blofield School, Blofield Post Office, the library and Garden Farm shop. We also venture further afield, to the Sea Life Centre and Norwich Castle Museum.

Blofield Playgroup continues to thrive, with spaces filled every year. Of the 31 children attending, some are the descendants of children who have attended in the past. At the time of writing, staff members include Gill Grand, Wendy Searle, Margaret Redhead and Tina Everson.

Blofield Nursery

The day nursery provides baby and toddler care and teaching for the pre-school years. It opened in 1994 and it is known by the children as the Pink House.

The Playgroup at Blofield Heath

When, in 1963, Petra Searle and some friends found that their four-year-old children who could not begin school needed the stimulation and company which a playgroup could provide, Petra set one up in her home:

Wendy Searle, Gill Grand, Margaret Redhead and Tina Everson with the children of the pre-school playgroup in 2005.

Children at Blofield Nursery learning about cleaning teeth with some dental nurses, 2005.

Healthlands Youth Club, 2006.

Norfolk Social Services inspected and approved us to take up to 11 under fives and with two adults always present. Sessions were from 9.30 to 12.30 three days a week. Mr Bacon at Blofield school gave us five 'infant' chairs and we even qualified for free milk!

When we closed in 1968, playgroups were springing up in most village halls. One was started in the tin hut which was then Blofield Heath Hall.

The present pre-school group meets in the space and comfort of Heathlands community centre, offering four half-day sessions and good links with Hemblington School.

Heathlands Youth Club
by Jackie Durrant

Some 13 years ago the present Heathlands Youth Club was a fledgling founded for the youth of the village, who had no out-of-school location in which to meet their friends safely.

Heathlands was founded by three people, Jackie Durrant, Suzanne Hughes and the late Steve Beaumont. Through the determination and dedication of these initial founders Heathlands Youth Club is an established part of the village community, a very successfully run club which meets twice a month, providing a valuable asset to Blofield Heath and surrounding areas for young people to meet in a safe environment.

Other initial helpers were Rosemary Gronco and Gary Starkings, who still helps.

In 2006 the club is run by Jackie, Suzanne, Gary, Doris and Tori, all of whom volunteer their time to keep the club going.

On a typical night the young people, and some of us older ones, can have a go on our trampoline, play pool, air hockey and table tennis, try disco board dancing or the Playstation, and we usually end the evening with a game of football. During the warmer months many a game of rounders is enjoyed on the field.

Leaders meet to work out activities and venues. This year (2006) we plan bowling, an Easter egg hunt – one of our traditions – and visits to Megazone and Hautbois House, where safe tuition is provided in such activities as rock climbing, canoeing and other outdoor pursuits.

When we stay at Heathlands there is always an extra activity, such as a camera and photography evening, quiz and chips or a craft evening. In other words, it is not just table tennis!

Over the last 13 years a group of dedicated people – Lily Barnes, Edith Chettleburgh and Edna James – have joined us voluntarily twice a year. Our regular supporters, who turn up every time, are much appreciated.

Our early members have enjoyed the youth club and moved on to adulthood with careers and families of their own. We feel privileged to know all our members, past and present; we keep in touch and take pride in all their achievements.

Girl Guides

In 1973 Ann Mills re-formed the First Blofield Guide Company. They met initially at the village school, where Eric Bacon sometimes allowed them use of the swimming pool. Soon Ann had an enthusiastic group of 36 girls enjoying badge work, games, experiencing outings and going to camp.

Ann's husband, Mike, worked with Lawrence Harding to train a group of Army Cadets.

Pat Seckerson offered to help with the Guides but Ann suggested that she form a Brownie pack of girls to feed into the Guide company.

Pat has spent 47 and a half years in uniformed Guiding.

Denise Bates leads the Brownies at Blofield Heath and a Rainbow group for younger girls is run in Blofield by Margaret Wright.

The re-formed Guide company with Brownies in 1974. Left to right, back row: ?, Sherry Bullen, Sally Gard, Fiona Jackson, Jane Powell, ?, Sara Basey-Fisher, ?, ?, Kim Bullen; third row: ?, Julie Thompson, Jane Hardy, Helen Fowler, Claire ?, Karen ?, Susan ?; second row: Alison Purdy, ?, Anne Lawrence, Diana Carman, Ann Mills, Sheila Mackintosh, Sarah Bishop, Amanda ?, Fenella Reid; front row: Tracey Dunmore, Sarah Carman, ?, Sandra Bullen, Carol Hague, Lorraine King, Elizabeth ?.

Guides at camp, c.1995.

At the suggestion of the Parish Council various village groups donated seats. Blofield Guides presented this at Bonfire Green in 1976. Left to right, back row: Pat Seckerson, Sally Gard, Sandra Bullen, Diana Carman, Ann Mills, Ken Pink; middle row, seated: Marjorie Ireland, Fred Ireland and John Taylor; standing: Helen Fowler, Louise Thomsett; front, sitting: Samantha Cole, ?, Helen Morley, ?.

Brownies and Rainbows at a Thinking Day event, 2006.

Scouts

The year 1914 was an exciting one for Blofield Boy Scouts. In June their new colours were dedicated by the Bishop of Thetford at a uniformed organisations' parade in church. The boys were congratulated on their very smart appearance by Major Crawley of the Twelfth Royal Lancers.

During August the boys attended a rally at Norwich, where their cooking was commended by the Chief Scout, Sir Robert Baden Powell, who 'tasted some of their tea and ate a potato with much satisfaction.'

The Boy Scouts were called upon by the government to watch telegraph wires to safeguard lines of communication across the country: 'They were in the place assigned to them within 24 hours, were on service for five days and received the thanks of the Post Office for their prompt assistance.'

Maurice Gardener became involved with Blofield Scouts soon after he moved here. By chance he met George Rope in the Globe and was introduced to his cousin from Canada, who said, 'Blofield Scout group? Look at this...', and took from his pocket two sepia photos. One showed a group of Scouts and the other the bishop of Thetford presenting the colours. He went away and had them copied in black and white and the names written beneath. They were presented to Maurice Gardener and the Scout group and hang in the ward room.

In 1970 Sea Scouts provided and delivered over 60 bags of kindling wood to old people in the Blofield and Brundall areas as their Christmas

Blofield Boy Scouts, 19 July 1919, with Canon Shillito in the garden of the rectory, now the Old Hall, opposite the church.

Boy Scouts at camp, 1953. Left to right, back row: *Brian Fuller, David Ferra, Ivan Forster, Michael Moore, Mr Ian Rowarth;* third row: *John Hornagold, Peter Rope, Brian Francis, Colin Andrews, Denis Wymer;* second row: *Geoffrey Gowing, John Howard, Derek Buxton;* front row: *Colin Debbage, Terence Murphy, Ian Greenhill, Michael Gilder.*

Royal Naval summer camp on board HMS Bristol, *2005.*

good turn. 'This is the true spirit of scouting,' remarked Mr M.V. Gardener.

The Wolf Cubs group was formed on 5 March 1942, when:

Miss Leeds from Norwich, Miss Cross from Brundall and some of the parents came to help Miss Helen Grass to 'kick off'. Mr Michael Royal is to act as treasurer. The Pack will meet every Thursday at 6pm at the Rectory.

The Red Cross

Margaret Harker joined the Red Cross in 1910 and set up a detachment at her home.

At the outbreak of the First World War she was offered the use of Brundall House as a war hospital, by its owner Mr ffiske, on condition that she was commandant. She directed the work of this hospital until October 1916. During the following years, as well as being county director, she supervised lectures, medical supplies, working parties and a blood transfusion service, and was president of the District Nursing Association and originator of the Linen Guild at the Jenny Lind Hospital. All this while bringing up four daughters!

Seeing a need for improved infant nutrition and medical care, she provided one of the first baby welfare clinics. Initially, this was in a wooden building near the school; a Red Cross Room was later built beside the parish hall. Here, babies were weighed, advice given and doctors were in attendance. She even arranged for transport for people from outlying places.

Attracting young members to the Red Cross was another of her ideas. Rallies were held at Blofield Hall, with many hundreds of children crowding the grounds from all parts of Norfolk. Competitions and sports were arranged for them and the rallies were looked forward to and enjoyed.

Red Cross activities for youngsters have continued to be a popular part of village life.

Lynne Janes (née Buxton) was a cadet. She remembers meeting on Monday evenings in the Red Cross Hut and the demonstrations of mouth-to-mouth resuscitation and bandaging and working for certificates and badges:

Blofield and Brundall Sea Scouts with Cubs and Beavers at Blofield Church harvest service, 2005. The leaders are Rusty Carter, Ann Kelly and John Kelly.

A group of Red Cross cadets show their Endeavour Trophy, won in 1980. Left to right, back row: Steven Chaplin, Kim Buxton, Graham Carter, Stuart Mackay, Karen Dyble, Jane Kirten, Jacky Emblem, Melanie George, Clive Chaplin; third row: Yvonne Goddard, Susan Griffin, Karen Batchelor, Julie Parker, Tina Hale, Sharon Tate, Suzanne Graveling, Susan Youngs, Sally Carter, Wendy Green; second row: Susan Law, Lynne Buxton, Susan Howard, Julie Hale, Mrs Rita Marriott, Sheila Dunstan, Celia Duffield, Linda Griffin; front row: Mark Marriott, James Batchelor, Philip Goddard, Joy Chaplin, Veronica Goddard, Bernice Monck.

We had work books, to learn from and work in, about first aid, home nursing, health and hygiene, infant and childcare and we took examinations.

Mrs Clamp, Mrs Burton and Mrs Marriott were the leaders involved.

We entered all-day competitions at Hellesdon, Yarmouth and Wymondham against other units.

Mrs Rita Marriott tells the story:

Once the cadets had gained their medallion for proficiency they could do duty in uniform at baby clinics, blood donor clinics, foot clinics for the elderly and they also attended fêtes, Great Yarmouth hippodrome, gymkhanas, picture houses and festivals as first aiders. So the medallion was very much sought after. The youngsters knew that good behaviour was expected and was indeed essential.

Competitions in schools throughout Norfolk each year were always entered by the Blofield cadets. Mock accidents would be staged involving different kinds of casualties at the same time. Teams of five or six cadets were expected to cope with them under the leadership of one senior cadet.

Rita took over the cadets from Miss Cubbitt of Brundall:

A marvellous lady who had served the Red Cross all through the Second World War. There were six girls. Two or three boys hung around the Red Cross Hut so we invited them in. That is how we started a mixed group.

Cadets helped at the Clare School for children with special needs:

They played wheelchair games and you can guess who won; not us!

In 1977 so many children under 11 wanted to join that we decided to get some help to form a younger Red Cross unit. Mrs Helen Dunn from Lingwood offered to do so and, along with Mrs Buxton, Lynne's mother, they began to meet. In 1979 four Blofield cadets won cadet of the year awards. Rosalyn Clamp, Lucy Henderson-Gray, Janet Hale and Lynne Buxton represented Blofield in London.

Soon there were 52 members in two groups aged between eight and 18 years.

They were happy times. Blofield can be really proud of what all these youngsters have achieved.

Blofield Silver Band

In 1982 Terry Ogden wrote:

In the winter of 1935 a stranger stepped purposefully

Blofield Silver Band during a visit to Yarmouth in 1948. Left to right, back row: *Bert Youngman, Aubrey Daynes, William Gould, Albert Grimes, Trevor Grimes, Ernie Nicholls, ?, Rex Barrett, Mike Gould;* front row: *Bob Barber, Harry Green, George Bailey, Mrs Green, Fred Howes, Billy Loades.*

from a train in Brundall and enquired of the ticket collector, 'Where be the local brass band?'

Was it the boldness of the question that struck our transport official dumb? Was it the forceful bearing of our stranger, his 'foreign' accent or simply the chill of the morning that persuaded momentarily the tongue of the railway man to rivet to the palate? Whatever it was, tense seconds elapsed as the eyes of the stranger bore into the, by now, confused official. Our stranger was not intimidated by what he deduced as local obduracy. Here was a man of determined mettle who could out-stubborn the most boorish of locals. 'Where be the band?'

Did our stranger hear the muffled reply correctly, 'Quarter past one'.

'There ent one? Well I better do somefin about it then.'

That stranger, Harry Green, strode up the hill towards the White Horse with now still greater purpose in his step. Blofield and District Silver Band was born in his mind.

Within a few months Harold had formed a band, requisitioned the Reading Rooms at Blofield as a head-quarters, bought a job lot of instruments, impressed players and instilled his indomitable spirit. Play anywhere, in any weathers, at any time (frequently also in any time many would say!) was the spirit.

Members of the band

George Bailey, a basket-maker at Hovells shop in Norwich, lived in the first cottage down North Street opposite the library.

Bertie Youngman used to play the last post at Armistice Day services in Blofield Church.

Sidney Saunders, who played solo cornet in the band in later years, recalls that Mrs Green played tenor horn and Sylvia Rayner the trombone. They played at a fête at Blofield Hall on an overcast day.

Sidney recalls:

Mr Futter, a minister at the Methodist chapel in Blofield Heath, was our conductor. As it came on to rain his baton flew faster and faster. Rather out of breath, we finished the piece just before the rain got really heavy.

CHAPTER 10

Memories

Many people have told me that they were born in such and such a house or cottage. How many of us nowadays can say, 'That's the house where I was born'?

Here are the recollections of a few of the people who have lived in our parishes.

Arthur Barber

Arthur came to Blofield, aged two, in 1918 and lived at Town Pit. His father, Arthur George Barber, had enlisted in the Norfolk Regiment in 1896 aged 18 and served in South Africa and the First World War.

He became a builder and once worked up Blofield Church tower replacing one of the stone figures. Young Arthur built his own house in Cuttons Corner. Sadly, his brother Benjamin was killed in the Second World War.

Arthur Browne, aged 93

In 1997 he wrote:

I am writing this to show how things have changed in my lifetime. I was born on Boxing Day in 1912 and am now in my eighty-fourth year. My birthplace was a little place called Wood Farm in the village of Pedham. When I was two years old we moved to another house in the village, where I lived till I got married in July 1936 at the age of 24.

I started school when I was four years old, and I had a mile to walk. When I was about seven or eight I went to live with my granny, who lived in the neighbouring village of Panxworth, and from there I had to walk just over three miles, no school buses in them days.

My father was a gamekeeper and he got called up for the Army in the First World War and was killed in 1916 when I was four years old. My mother was left with three boys and another on the way and she had a hard time bringing us up, but we all survived. We used to have porridge for breakfast and we had good old suet dumplings, jam roly-poly, things which today people dare not eat for fear of getting fat.

I left school when I was 14. It was Christmas and I started work on the farm as that was the only job going at the time. My first job was to take a horse and tumbril to the field to collect swedes, and I can tell you it was a jolly cold job. When I got older I went to plough with two horses and I liked that very much. There used to be five of us ploughing in the same field and that was a lovely sight to see, all those horses going up and down the field. Now there is not one horse on the farm, all tractors.

Arthur Browne's family outside their house at the bottom of Hemblington Hill, c.1927. Left to right: Tony, Harry Knights (step-father) with Hilda, George, Ethel (mother) with Doris, Arthur, Jimmy, Harry.

Threshing directly from the field at Hemblington.

When I started work I was only getting 10s. (50p) so after mother took her share I did not have much to spend. I bought a bike on the hire purchase and I paid 1s. a week for it. As I got older I went to work for the men hoeing sugar beet and mangolds and this was piecework so I earned a little more money. There used to be ten or 12 men hoeing, now there is not one hoe used, all machines.

After the hoeing came the hay making. Now there are no horses so they do not want the hay. Next came the harvest. We cut the corn with horses on the binder which tied the corn into bundles called sheaves. These we picked up and stood up in rows round the field. This was very tiring as we went from seven in the morning till nine o'clock at night. See anyone doing that today! Today one man can combine a large field in a day; what a change. There were about ten or 12 men on the farm then, today there are only two, all machinery. We had about 15 large stacks of corn, oats, wheat and barley. They stood till the winter months, when they were threshed out one at a time. A threshing machine used to travel round the farms and it took all day to do one stack.

When I was 18 I got a full man's pay, which was 30s., £1.50, a week and I continued on that until I was married. So you can see I could not save much money.

After the corn harvest came the sugar beet harvest. We had to dig them up and cut off the tops. They were then carted off to the factory at Cantley for processing into sugar. Now one man can do a whole field of sugar beet all alone with a machine.

I never thought I would see so many changes. We did not have any bank holidays in them days nor annual holidays. If it was a wet day and you could not work you lost a day's pay. When I was 23 years old I married a girl I went to school with. Hilda was her name and we lived in a little cottage called Cherry Tree Cottage in Blofield. I never did see a cherry tree, though. A year after we were married Geoffrey was born on 7 July 1937. We lived in Blofield for two years, then we moved back to Hemblington.

When I started work my boss went to Norwich every Saturday in a horse and cart. There were no cars about our way then. Farmers would race each other to see who had the fastest horse. After a few years he bought an old Ford which everyone called 'the old tin Lizzie' but now of course farmers have two or three posh cars in the yard.

There are many things that have changed, such as washing. It was done in a bath with water heated in a copper in the wall with a fire underneath and all the water had to be cranked up from a well outside. Now we put the clothes in a washing machine and sit down till it's done. Another thing we had to do was go outside to the toilet, which was a little shed down the garden and that in winter was not very nice. Now we go in the little room indoors and sit in the warm as long as you like. We used to get up in the mornings to a very cold room and the first thing was clear out the ashes from the grate. This was a messy job. Then you lit the fire and it was a long time before you felt any heat. Now we get up in the morning to nice central-heated rooms.

For several years we never had any music in our house, then mother bought a gramophone and a few records and we did enjoy playing that in the evenings, but compared with today's music it was very poor. Now we have radio and television with music of the highest quality. This is all about changes in my lifetime.

When I was a boy we used to spin tops all the way to school in the middle of the road, no fear from cars but now it's hardly safe to walk on the path. What it will be like in years to come I shudder to think. Mother used to bake all the bread in the oven in the wall. Now I don't suppose many people know how to make nice bread. Today it is nothing like as good. It was lovely coming home from school and having a shortcake hot from the oven. When we were children we would go in the harvest field and have lots of fun chasing the rabbits when they were cutting the corn. Now children are not allowed in the fields as it is too dangerous with all the machinery.

We went to chapel Sunday school in the mornings and church Sunday school in the afternoons. The reason for going to both was in the summer we had two excursions to Yarmouth, one for each. They were the only treats we had.

I forgot to say my mother married again and we had two sisters and another brother, that made seven of us in the family; big families in them days. When I was a teenager I went to Norwich to the pictures, as we called them then, now they are films. They were silent pictures. I used to sit in the ninepennies, all I could afford, and I was very excited when the talkies came.

In September 1939 the Second World War started. On 20th November Kathleen was born. As I worked on the farm I was in a reserved occupation so I did not get called up for National Service. I joined what was called the Home Guard. We were equipped with rifles and ammunition and we patrolled the roads at night and after working all day it was very tiring. I did not mind as I was doing something. One night we had a bad air raid in Norwich and Jerry dropped two bombs very close to our house and the shrapnel from the bombs cut through the electricity cable that went over the road leading up to the farm and it set the hedges on both sides *of the road alight. I went running up to see if I could help put it out and stood on the high tension cable and it quickly put me out of action. Everyone said it was a miracle I was not killed. It was a nasty sensation but I got over it. There was an American airbase nearby and in the mornings about seven o'clock they would take off and fly over our house one after another, getting ready for their daily bombing mission over Germany. There were over 40 American airbases all over East Anglia and the bombers would fly around till they got together in one mass formation. It was a thrilling sight to see. After they had formed they would then go off on their mission. People won't believe us when we tell them we have counted over 1,000 planes all flying off to bomb Germany. The Americans bombed by day and the RAF at night, so you can see how many planes, including Germans. During and after the war we were rationed for food and clothing so we had to go very sparingly with everything.*

After the war I thought I would like to change my job so I got a job at Drayton as a cowman, but I did not stop there very long as I could not get on with the head cowman. That is another big change, when milking was all done by hand. It is now done by machine and one man can milk 40 or 50 cows all on his own. Well, I went back to my old boss and I went feeding bullocks. I liked that job because it was inside in the dry all winter.

When my boss retired from the farm I got another job as a porter at Little Plumstead Hospital. It was a bit different but not so hard work and I was getting quite a lot more money than I had been getting. I was there till I retired at 65, finishing up as a supervisor.

After I retired it seemed a bit strange getting up in the morning at any time I liked and having the day to do what I liked instead of being told what to do. It was very nice. I used to go for long cycle rides and some-times we, that is Hilda and I, would get the bus to Yarmouth or somewhere. I had a large garden and as I liked gardening I spent a lot of my time there. Since I retired there has been a big change in the village. I think I can honestly say they have built over 300 houses. It's the same in my old village of Hemblington.

January 2006
I am now started on my ninety-fourth year and seem to be in a different world to the one I've written about, the one I was born into. The hustle and bustle of everything going so fast. As I said before we never saw a car, now there's thousands. Another thing, we could go out and leave the door unlocked and never had to worry, we knew everyone in the village, not now.

Olive Conlin (née Hanton) aged 80

George London had a hut where he sold shoes at one end, in the middle groceries and sweets, aprons, slippers and so on at the other. At the back he sold paraffin and made ice-cream. He came round with a sidecar on Saturday mornings and sold a halfpenny cornet or a penny wafer.

Old Mrs Marriott had the sweet shop at the old Post Office. She sold shoe leather and things like that and at the back Norman used to mend bikes and there were chains and other bike bits and pieces there.

As a little girl Olive used to go and stand up near the Globe:

I think it would be just after Easter. The fair used to leave Norwich and there would be horses with their tails braided pulling all the fairground things and we'd stand there nearly all day watching this procession go through from Norwich to Yarmouth.

Phyllis Cutler

Phyllis Cutler, later Jermy, born 1921, grew up in Hemblington:

Families lived close by, they didn't think of moving away.
We made our own fun. I was out of the village but there were one or two girls nearby. We used to play on grandfather's pasture, leapfrog and that sort of thing. I loved to play netball.
In winter they used to let us out of school a little bit early but it was still dark when we got home.
At Christmas time at school the partition was pulled back and we had a stage for a performance.

Phyllis remembers sad times at the Post Office:

I can remember Mr Webb's daughter Ruby dying; it stuck in my mind. She was very, very ill and they were trying to keep things quiet and they laid all straw outside on the road for the traffic that went past. She wasn't very old, only a teenager or early 20s. That stuck in my mind; the sadness.

Kenny Foulger

Kenny Foulger was born in 1920:

At Blofield school we went to the 'rec' for games lessons, then a piece of land at the end beyond the carpentry block was bought for a playing-field.
The master, Mr Foreman, made malt for the children to drink.
Once a week there were lessons in carpentry and gardening. An area was divided into strips and boys were responsible for digging it and planting crops. I didn't think I needed lessons, because I had about an acre at home.

He and his mother, Alice Foulger, kept poultry where they lived opposite Rotten Row. The man who lived next door worked as a saddler at the Turret House.

His mother, born in 1883, was a pupil teacher at Blofield School, then looked after the library in the Reading Room. New books arrived from the County once or twice a year and were kept in the back room until someone made her a cabinet to hold them.

The Globe bowling green, c.1870.

Ken remembers:

Gwen Shillito taught the cubs. She was friendly with Rosamund Harker, who was a rally driver. She drove great big cars, she had a Bentley! The cubs went once to Yarmouth. 'Boys, do you want to go fast?' she asked. We went at 100mph on the Acle Straight. We loved every minute of it. We didn't do it that long but we did reach 100mph.

Dr Heathcote Statham used to come to test the choristers. Stanley Trett, Maurice and Ronnie Marshall and Alan Merrison were all in the choir with Ken, and they sat in one particular stall in the chancel.

As a choirboy Ken went to Lingwood workhouse to sing carols.

I will never forget it. There was a huge stove and these poor old people were sitting huddled round it and we had to sing carols. I'll remember it the rest of my days. Poor old people.

The bowling green at the Globe was beautiful. The boys used to wipe clean the bowls for the players.

Violet Hubbard

Violet Hubbard, later Wicks, now aged 85, was born in a cottage near Hemblington Hall. Her father worked for Mr Youngs as a bullock feeder. She used to play at the Hall with Mr Youngs' grandchildren, and she passed the mill on her way to school.

The school day began at 9am with a break from 10.45 to 11, there was no milk then, and we came home at 3.45. I walked to school. In winter it was a dark walk. I

didn't have a bike till I was about 11 and then I cycled to school till I was 14.

In wet weather your clothes were hung up in the porch and were still wet when you put them on to walk home. You sat in class in damp clothes too.

By the time we got home it was time for our teas. Nearly time for bed.

There were outings sometimes:

We went to Yarmouth; by lorry to Brundall Station, train to Yarmouth then steam boat to Gorleston to have our dinners.

I left school at 14 to go to my first job down Doctors Road where I lived in. I felt homesick at first, however there were two girls where I worked and they said I was more of a companion. I was really lucky; the family took me out with them. I stayed 7 years with them. I would come home on half days and Sundays to my mother.

Home life
We had no electricity in our house in Hemblington, just a lamp on the table and candles to go to bed. On the upstairs landing mother had a little lamp burning all night. It was cold upstairs. Our toilet was outside so you didn't want to go at night.

Washing
Mother had lines and lines and lines of white sheets. There were five of us children and mother took in washing too.

Shopping
Hardly Symonds was the shoe mender near the chapel on Woodbastwick Road. Bailey also repaired shoes at No. 63 Mill Road in a shed.

Vans came round; Blake from South Walsham came on Tuesday, Rix of Acle on Friday and the fish man came to the gate. Mr L.T. Clamp, the butcher from South Walsham, called on his rounds.

Phyllis Neave also recalls Mr Coe, the baker from Salhouse, delivering bread and cakes; Mr Money from Coltishall came on a Friday and Roys of Wroxham delivered shopping each week, collecting a list of the following week's needs.

Violet's husband worked for Roys after the war. She helped out with the delivery round and did the books and orders.

Clothes

A pack man came round once a fortnight on a Tuesday after tea. He carried a bag and sold all sorts of clothes. The boys liked to choose neckties and scarves.

Mother was in a clothes club; you went to Butchers in Norwich for school clothes.

Wireless

The first wirelesses had accumulators. These were brought round fortnightly by Beales of Lingwood. Gramophones had a big horn and were wound up.

Marion Jackson (née Knights), 1920–2004

Every year a fair came to the village. The fair people made bread and we children took it for them to Kahler's bakery to have it baked. The reward would be a penny ticket to go to the fair. In the marquee were puppet shows, dogs and other small animals. It was very exciting to children.

Alice Brown and Marion both commented that their mothers never went away anywhere except on church and chapel outings. Marion played at home with mud pies but really looked forward to the sand and 'playing with clean muck' when she went to the seaside.

Arthur Jermy

Arthur Jermy was born in 1926 at Acle, one of twins:

My father was a stockman at Hall Farm, Hemblington, and my father was given a rent free, semi-detached cottage at Wood Farm.

My earliest recollections are of about 1931 when I was five years old.

The cottages consisted of two rooms downstairs and two upstairs. There was a large living-room and a kitchen with a walk-in pantry. The floors were of red brick and there was an open fireplace in the living-room. In the kitchen was a fireplace with hobs each side for cooking pots. There was also an iron copper set in brickwork with a fire underneath for washing clothes; also an oven in the wall. The front bedroom was quite large; the back bedroom was smaller and restricted because of the sloping roof. Each cottage had a large garden with a path leading to the lavatory, the privy, and an adjoining shed in which were stored coal, vegetables, garden tools and bicycles. There was no indoor sanitation and the distance from the house to the privy was about 30 yards. Water was obtained from a well in my grandparents' garden.

The cottages were owned by the farmer, Mr Alfred John Youngs, who lived at Hemblington Hall.

On Hemblington Hill there were three cottages joined in a strange irregular fashion and a detached cottage joined to a thatched smithy. A travelling blacksmith used it periodically until the mid-1930s.

About 100 yards from our house were two large barns and stockyards where bullocks were fattened during the winter.

Self-sufficient

Wood Farm was quite isolated and tradesmen were reluctant to face the long lane from the metalled road to the cottages, inches deep in mud for most of the winter. However, we had little need for travelling salesmen as we were virtually self sufficient in foodstuffs. In the large garden we grew enough potatoes to last all year and many other vegetables in season. We had apple, plum and pear trees and a variety of soft fruits with which my mother made jam. She also baked all the bread we needed. My father caught rabbits on the farm and there were not many weeks when rabbit was not on the menu. He sold the surplus for sixpence each to his friend Mr Laurence Clamp, the butcher at South Walsham. Our food was also supplemented with chestnuts and hazelnuts from the woods nearby and mushrooms, which grew in abundance in season on nearby meadows. A large amount of our fuel came from the nearby woods and my brother and I spent many hours sawing logs and chopping kindling, often by moonlight.

We had no electricity at Wood Farm and used oil-lamps and candles. A delivery van brought the Eastern Weekly Press *on Saturday evenings and also paraffin from a tank on the van. This came as far as Hemblington Hill. My twin sister and I, from about the age of eight years, often tramped across the fields armed with a large paraffin can and a candlelit lantern to collect the oil and papers.*

I attended Yarmouth Grammar School, which was evacuated to Retford in Nottinghamshire in 1940, and I stayed there until I left school in 1943.

George 'Tiddler' Mackerell

George 'Tiddler' Mackerell was born in 1927 in the family cottage at Frogs Hole, now named Shack Lane. He weighed 2½lbs at birth and was put in a shoebox and wrapped in cotton wool. The doctor said that if he made it to seven years old he would be the biggest in the family.

He began school in 1932 and stayed until he was 14. At school he remembers a garden at the side, down to the hedge where the doctor lives now, where gardening skills were taught: 'Gardening, bee keeping and chickens so that you could learn how to look after them and sell the eggs and so on.' Towards the end of George's time at Blofield School a fence was put across the playground, dividing the boys' from the girls' sides.

He remembers the Walls ice-cream man coming and standing outside the school with a three-wheeler bike.

Graham Martin

Graham Martin, who grew up in Hemblington, recalls Jack Cutler the son of Pedham's gamekeeper.

The school teacher asked Jack which of two birds, the moorhen or the coot, had webbed feet. His reply was 'Neither'. 'You should know better than that being a gamekeeper's son,' she retorted, and after the ensuing argument she finished up caning him twice on each hand with a ruler. However next day he arrived at school and threw two birds on her desk which he had shot the night before, a moorhen and a coot, from observation of which it could be seen neither had webbed feet. He was told to take them away and nothing else was said. Can you imagine such an incident taking place today?

John Richards

John Richards came to Hemblington in 1941, when his father came to work for Mr Godfrey Weston as horseman.

We moved from Southrepps by lorry with the furniture covered with a tarpaulin. The cottage we lived in was one of two on the corner of Hemblington Hall Road and Cinder Muck Lane (this led across to Pedham). I was four and went to Hemblington School from the age of five until we moved away in 1946. The headmaster was Mr Watson. Virol and malt were handed out at school to keep us all healthy. Farm workers were given extra rations of essential groceries, I think two or three times a year.

I remember my father ploughing the field opposite our house; two horses and a single-furrow plough. I went with my mother pea picking on the farm; we knelt on the ground, stripped the pods off the vine and put them in a sack. These we weighed and the pickers paid us accordingly. People were transported from Norwich to help with this.

Steam-drawn threshing tackle came to thresh the stacks. Netting was put round the stack on threshing day so that rats and mice could not escape and were killed, often by dogs.

I took father his tea to the field at harvest and sugar beet hoeing time. We all sat on the bank of the hedge and shared the food. It always seemed like one big picnic to the children.

I can remember seeing a bus painted grey, No. 7B, instead of the usual red. This was fuelled by gas, which was on a trailer behind the bus.

On Sunday afternoon I can recall going on my bike with father and sitting by the main road hoping to see some cars!

Ivy Ryan (née Whittaker)

Ivy Ryan was born in Cuttons Corner in 1914 and her parents lived there until she was seven years old.

As a child she had one dress for school, which came to below the knees, and one for the Sunday-school anniversary at chapel, where she did recitations. She had to learn them and perform them sometimes alone, sometimes in a group, sometimes with her three sisters.

Over the dress, to keep it clean, she wore a white pinafore which was washed and boiled by her mother. She wore knee-length socks with garters and ankle-length lace-up boots, which were repaired by the village shoemaker. She wore a hat – a tammy in winter and a sun hat in summer.

Often her sisters' clothes were handed down but there was a clothing club at the Methodist chapel. Her mother paid in each week and then, in September or October, she got the money and went to Butchers to spend it. One winter, when she was 12, Ivy had a coat with a huge collar. That was the year she got scarlet fever and spent six weeks upstairs. There was a piece of string out of the window so she could pull up food and presents, oranges and the like. Her mother came to see her but no visitors, and a disinfectant sheet hung over the door to keep the germs in.

Ivy's mother's busy week
Monday: *To do the washing she lit the fire. Dad filled the copper from the tanks of soft water from the roof. Cottons were washed in one bath, washed in a second bath, put into the copper to boil, put into clear water in bath one, into blue water in bath two and through the mangle, which sat in the bath.*

Colours did not go into the copper, they were washed in two baths, rinsed in two baths, mangled and hung outdoors or on ropes across the room after the children were in bed

Tuesday *was ironing day. Suits were brushed and put away and two heaters for ironing were put in the fire. The heater was a block of cement, triangular, like a wedge of cheese. When it was hot you put it with tongs into the box which was the iron and closed the little door. Then you were ready to iron. Another heater would be ready to use when the first had cooled down. It took all morning to do the ironing then the clothes were aired on an airing horse round the fire or hung on the fireguard.*

Wednesday *was needlework and mending day.*

On **Thursday** *mother cleaned the bedrooms, sweeping them out.*

Friday *was cleaning downstairs day, using a brush and dustpan, shaking rugs, sweeping and polishing the floor.*

On **Saturday** *she went to Norwich to shop and on* **Sunday** *she cooked lunch, roast meat for father, beef, pork or lamb.*

Mother was a good cook, making apple tarts and her own bread and buns in an oven in the wall. Monday's meal was cold meat, as she had no time to cook.

Mother made sandwiches or brought hot soup to school in a can for the children. Dad was a County Council borough surveyor. He went round smallholdings, made repairs and wrote specifications. My brother, Tom, worked under his Dad.

Mrs Sharman (née Gotts)

Now in her ninety-fourth year, in 1929 Muriel Gotts went to Blofield School as a student teacher. Mr Foreman was headmaster and Mrs Rope, the infant teacher, was a very nice person.

The school had four rooms, one large with a partition and two smaller rooms. Desks were double with lifting lids and joined seats. Infants had tables and chairs. At 9 o'clock each morning the bell rang, children lined up and marched into their rooms. Lessons were 30 minutes long with playtime morning and afternoon. Most children went home for dinner, those who lived too far away brought sandwiches. A few mothers brought their children to school others came in groups. The school nurse came to inspect heads. Children who had ringworm would have their hair closely cropped and wear a kind of mob cap for warmth.

She later attended the teacher-training college in College Road in Norwich, which was burned down in the war by incendiary bombs.

Cecil Sharman, her husband, was taught by Miss Mower at Blofield School. He wrote with his left hand but she would not allow this and cured him of it by rapping his knuckles with a knitting needle every time he used his left hand.

Bertie Skedge

Bertie Skedge was chairman of Blofield Parish Council for many years. Skedge Way was named in recognition of his services. Bertie's daughter, Nancy Mills, recalls:

My grandfather, Charles Skedge, 1867–1952, was one of eight children and he had to pay a penny to go to school at Blofield. He married Hannah Feek from Pedham and had only one child, Bertie, my Dad.

When I was born they lived at Field Lane Farm. He was farm steward of that farm and on another one at Pedham, two of the several owned by Myrus Sutton.

He would visit the Pedham farm in his horse and cart, with our dog Scot, several times a week. He was very religious, read the Bible every day, and attended the little chapel at Cuttons corner.

I believe he was quite hard to live with and we weren't allowed to knit on Sundays, and had to sing hymns when we had a ride in the horse and cart.

Dad was Bertie Richard Skedge (1902–72). He was well educated for those times; he went to City of Norwich school and had a very good head for figures. He married Marjorie in 1930 and they moved into

No. 1 Laundry Lane, Blofield Corner. I, my sister Molly and brother Neville were born there.

When Nanny Hannah died about 1935, we moved down to the farm at Field Lane to look after Grandad. It had no electricity, no bathroom, the toilet was yards away down the end of the garden. There was a big kitchen with a black range and an oven in the wall. When Dad met Mr Underdown he had a job for life. He worked from the office behind Underdown's garage running the fleet of 14 lorries. It was mainly farm transport, sugar beet to the Cantley factory, corn etc., also gravel and stone for driveways. Later this became Edward J. Edwards.

During the war Dad was in the Auxiliary Fire Service. That was his war effort. Mum's was selling National Savings stamps all round Blofield Corner on her bike.

We went to Hemblington School. The teachers were Miss Bailey, Miss Jordan, and Mrs Snelling. There were coal fires and big fireguards. The bottles of free school milk had little cardboard tops with a hole to press to put your straw in. These stood in front of the fire to melt the ice on top. There were no school dinners and the toilets were out in the back playground. We wrote with scratchy pens dipped in inkwells and had desks with a lift up lid to keep our books in. The playtimes were fun; we played skipping with long ropes, two to turn it and the rest skipping in the middle, 'What's the time Mr Wolf?', ball games, of course, and in the winter, when it snowed, we had huge long slides in the playground.

Webbs shop and Post Office was where we spent our Saturday sixpence on 2oz of sweets from tall glass jars, pear drops, acid drops, aniseed balls, gobstoppers, coconut ice or perhaps a writing book and a pencil. We had a pork butcher in Mill Road who sold pies, sausages and pork scratchings, which were delicious.

What is now the Community Centre, was always called 'the hut' and the playing-field was 'the rec'. All our social events were at the hut. One of the first I remember was 1937 Coronation day. We have a photo of us in fancy dress, red white and blue flags and a gold cardboard crown on our heads. Lots of fêtes with games and teas in the hut. There were evenings which were called Socials! These were like party nights, with Mr Eric Martin from Pedham as MC, what a character he was.

About 1943 Mr Watson, the headmaster at Hemblington School, started the Methodist youth club in the hut for teenagers. We had games, discussions and, I think, table tennis. I don't remember all the names, the Stapleton girls Doreen and Beryl, Hazel Norton, Eric and Ronnie Dawson.

Later on we joined the GFS, Girls' Friendly Society, held in the Margaret Harker Hall and run by Miss Cubitt, who lived in Brundall. We did a lot of marching as well as dancing.

On special days we went on church parade along with the Red Cross, British Legion, Scouts, etc. There was always an amazing atmosphere of patriotism and the hymns, like 'O Valiant Heart' sung in a church packed full with people and banners.

HEMBLINGTON AND NORTH BLOFIELD

CORONATION CELEBRATION

WEDNESDAY, MAY 12th, 1937

Blofield Heath Recreation Ground

2 p.m. Fancy Dress Parade and Competition for Children and
        Adults. Prizes given. Followed by Children's Sports.
        Prizes given. Music provided by V. W. Henry, of
        Acle, Radio Engineers.

4 p.m. Feast for Adults in Marquee. Admission by Ticket only.
        PLEASE BRING KNIFE, FORK AND SPOON !

4 p.m. Tea for Children in Hemblington School, followed by
        Entertainment for Children to 6.30 p.m.

7 p.m. Social Evening commences in Hemblington School.
        Coronation Speeches, including that of H.M. the King.
        Entertainment and Dancing.

Residents who have not obtained a Feast Admission Ticket by Saturday, 1st May,
should apply to A. D. Babington, Hemblington School.

Coronation celebrations, 1937.

In about 1943 and 1944 there were some excellent shows and Concerts in Margaret Harker Hall. They were called 'The Norfolk Turkeys'. A lot of the actors and singers were professionals who were in the Forces stationed around the area. The standard was so good, especially the drama.

The summers were hotter and longer, the summer holidays spent in the harvest fields, playing around the stooks, chasing rabbits with sticks when the binder got to the middle of the field, the dogs usually got them. Lots of rabbit pies and stews to eke out the rations.

Peter Smith

Born in 1924, Peter Smith moved to Blofield in 1932 when his father, Obadiah Smith, became postmaster. Another unusual name in the family was Odesimah.

Peter remembers that school carpentry and cookery lessons were in a wooden hut. The boys used to get the sawdust and mix it in with the flour.

In the early 1930s a cricket match between an all Edrich 11 and a Falcon 11 was broadcast on the BBC Light Programme. Peter and his friends were at the match, and when someone hit a six they would dash into the house to hear it described on the radio!

Peter did deliveries for his father. Blofield Hall had a big front entrance and a rather overgrown back one. There were strict instructions that tradesmen should use the back way in, but if Peter ever went to deliver a telegram he took great delight in approaching by the grand front driveway. The Post Office rule was that telegrams could be delivered by any route!

Childhood games were often in the Street, only moving occasionally if a car came along – there was not much traffic about.

Boys used to get a long length of rope and tie it to the front door of Honor House and the other end to Marshalls, on the other side of the Street. Then they would pull it to knock on both doors before running to hide. When either householder tried to open their door they couldn't because of the tight rope.

Charlie Howes and David Woodrow playing in the Post Office yard, c.1935.

Roy Snelling

In 1954 Roy Snelling began what is now the biggest TV rental and sales company between Norwich and the sea.

As a small boy he was interested in electricity and magnetism. He attended Hemblington School, which was a mile from where he lives now and a mile from where he was born. The whole of his life he has 'moved round a field, that's all'.

On leaving school at 14 all he wanted to do was work with the wireless. An apprenticeship was followed by service in the Royal Electrical and Mechanical Engineers (REME), known to generations as Ruin Everything Mechanical Eventually. He returned, on his discharge, to repairing wireless sets and gramophones, the ultimate in home entertainment for many people.

In 1954, supported by his mother, he bought a redundant laundry for his business premises. Working seven days a week, usually for 16 hours at a stretch, he built up his business. He spent busy days adjusting sets, often calling at 10 o'clock at night to effect a repair.

Roy broke new ground as a TV supplier. In those days there was little choice; it was BBC TV switched on or BBC TV switched off.

Roy married and gladly delegated the growing office work to his capable wife Sheila, who joined him in working till late at night. After her death he turned the company into a charitable trust to protect the future employment of his staff and to ensure continuity of service to his many customers.

A deeply religious man, Roy has contributed much to the community, often in quiet, unobtrusive ways.

The business continues to move ahead of the times, with more and more technology. In 2004 Roy celebrated his eightieth birthday and 50 years of R.C. Snelling's business.

Norris Waterson

Norris Waterson's father, who lived in Pedham near the dam, carted hay using a cart pulled by a billy goat. Norris was born in 1934 at Town Pit in No. 3, where his parents had moved when the house was new. He attended Hemblington School.

When Norris was courting his future wife she would catch a bus over from Ranworth and later he would settle her on the box of his three-wheeler, wrapped up warmly, and drive her home.

At the time of writing, they have lived for 46 years in the house he built in Blofield Corner Road. He used to keep goats and bees and now has ducks, chickens, rabbits, budgies, finches and fish, and grows vegetables and fruit in profusion.

Spanton's outing to Little Plumstead Hall, 1914.

An outing organised by Billy Bugden, late 1940s. The picture includes, from left to right: *Mrs Batley, Mrs Andrews, Violet Hubbard, Michael Andrews, Billy Curtis, Mrs Horace Webb, Russell Andrew, Colin Andrews, Alec Barber, Louis Hylton, Mabel Hylton, Eric Martin, Rusty Bugden, Mrs Barber, Mrs Ellie Bugden, Billy Barber, Kenny Hylton.*

CHAPTER 11

Events

Through the years our community has seen many events where folk have enjoyed themselves alongside their fellow villagers, whether it be cottagers' shows with competitions in country and domestic skills, fairs at the Globe Inn with bands and swing boats in the 1890s or concerts in the school-room or Reading Room.

Blofield's Michaelmas Fair

Peter Eade (1825–1915), who grew up in Blofield, recalled:

At this time there was an annual Fair held in Blofield 'Street,' at Michaelmas-time. It was on a very small scale, and consisted of three or four canvas-covered stalls for the sale of sweets and small articles, with one or two 'round-abouts' or other opportunities for the amusement of the younger part of the population. But, small as was the means of entertainment, this fair was largely attended.

A Village Celebrates

In the early 1900s dances and New Year parties were held in the Granary in Church Road; on one occasion 'a family party with a family of 250!' took place, with 60 of the 'family's' children being entertained at the same time in the Reading Rooms. There were outings for schools, churches, chapels, choirs, bell-ringers, sports groups and the special coach outings organised by Mr Martin at Hemblington. Time off together to relax and enjoy a change of scene.

From their opening in the 1920s the two recreation grounds held annual fêtes involving an enormous amount of planning and intriguing numbers of attractions. With a cessation only during the war these continued into the 1970s.

Queen Elizabeth II's jubilee year, 2002, saw celebrations on Blofield's rec. with sports for all ages followed by a quiz evening and a dance in the hall.

The Margaret Harker hall has seen films, dances,

Shooting party in the Hangings, 1950. Left to right: Jock Greer, Arthur Edrich, Edwin Edrich, Gwen Edrich, dog, Peter Edrich, Brenda Bircham, Ivan Watts, Charlie Bates, Cecil Merrison, Roy Everard, Pluto (the dog), F. Gunns, Frank Rope, George Edrich, Mrs Arthur Edrich (Midge), John Ingliss, Harold Becksfield.

A Village Fete in Blofield, 1951: Programme of Events

2.30 p.m.   *OPENING CEREMONY by Mr Norman Low, Manager of Norwich City Football club.*
2.45 p.m.   *PRIZE FANCY-DRESS PARADE for children of school age, representing Characters of Empire*
3.15 p.m.   *BABY SHOW. In three classes: (1) Up to six months (2) Six months to two years (3) Two years to four years. Prizes in each class (if not less than four entries): 3/-, 2/-, 1/-*
3.45 p.m.   *WATTS NAVAL SCHOOL GYMNASTICS DISPLAY (1)*
4.15 p.m.   *DISTRIBUTION OF PROGRAMME PRIZES FROM THE AIR. Special display of low-level flying.*
4.45 p.m.   *WATTS NAVAL SCHOOL GYMNASTICS DISPLAY (2)*
5.15p.m.   *AUCTION of Home produce Show Exhibits*
        HOME PRODUCE SHOW organised by the Blofield Woman's Institute. Schedules available from MISS HOGG, CHURCH ROAD, Blofield, or at The Post Office, Blofield.
        Target Bowls Competition   Lawn Tennis Tournament
        EXHIBITION FLIGHTS OF POWER DRIVEN MODEL AIRCRAFT will be given at various intervals throughout the afternoon
        TEAS will be on sale in the hall and FRUIT DRINKS and ICES on the Recreation Ground
        Other attractions include A CAKE STALL, JUMBLE STALL, HOUSEHOLD STALL, BRING-AND-BUY STALL and MANY SIDESHOWS.
8.0 p.m.   *GRAND CARNIVAL DANCE in the Margaret Harker Hall, Spot Prizes, Novelties, etc.*

pantomimes, plays and home-made entertainment.

Both schools held centenary events in 1978 and their annual summer fêtes and fairs attract large crowds.

The churches' and chapels' flower festivals, dislays of local arts and crafts and teddy bears parachuting rom Blofield's tower attract young and old alike from the parishes and further afield.

A fête at Blofield Heath recreation ground, c.1930.

Members of the Blofield Girls' Friendly Society enacting 'Britannia' at the Black Friars' hall in Norwich in 1938.
Left to right: *Stella Bracey, ?, Marjorie Howes, Molly Rose, Verdun Pitchers, Joyce Cann, ?, ?.*

Parade in Blofield Street during the First World War.

Revd Cassidy and Mrs Jackson organised village plays in the Margaret Harker Hall. Here, schoolchildren perform in the pantomime Snow White and the Seven Dwarfs, *January 1978. Left to right, back row: Jeremy Mills, Richard Hardy, Lesley Glass, Yvonne Wymer, Sally Mackintosh, Kerry Tai, Donna Jackson, Sally Gard, Joanne Evans, ?, Sarah Basey-Fisher; back row of dwarfs: Jeremy Monck, Adrian Hollis and Jane Hardy; front row: Claire Simmons, Anthea Simmons, ?, Neil Mackintosh, Sarah Carman and Darren Prior.*

Party for the retirement of Mr Smith, the postmaster, in the Margaret Harker Hall, 1960. Left to right, standing: ?, Marion Futter, Anna ?, ?, Jane Rowland, Jamie Macdonald, ?, ?, ?, ?, Janet Smith, Mr Smith, ?, Kenneth Hardy, Mrs Smith, Ruth Stone, Alan Lockwood, ?, Alma Layt, ?, ? Rope, Hilary Drake, ?, ?, John Grass; front: Ian Carter, John Green, ?, Elizabeth Jermy, Maria Culley.

'Mr and Mrs Brett, who lived from the 1930s to the 1970s at the White House, used to open their gardens for fêtes and tea parties held for local children.' Mrs Goldsmith remembers playing in the gardens. Pictured here, a church garden party with the silver band at the White House, 1986, with Mary and Sydney Lee in the foreground.

Members of the parish council planting a Whitebeam tree at the junction of St Andrew's Way and Yarmouth Road in memory of Diana, Princess of Wales, January 1999. Left to right: Shirley Rose, Pat Barnes, Glenna Butler, Sarah Russen, James Russen, Michael Sowerby, Roy Fowler.

Subscribers

James W. Anderson, Blofield, Norfolk

Vanessa Angier, Corpusty, Norfolk

C. and J. Ashman, Blofield Heath

Brian D. Askham, Norwich, Norfolk

Julie Atkins, Blofield, Norfolk

The Austin Family, Swan Cottage, Blofield, Norfolk

Barbara Ayers, Brundall, Norfolk

R. and D. Bailey, Rackheath, Norfolk

Daphne A. Baker (née Whittaker)

Mrs H. Bakker (née Cann), Lingwood

Mrs Catherine Barber, Blofield Heath, Norfolk

Mrs Lyn Barford, North Walsham

Barbara (née Trett) and Lionel Barker, Brundall, Norfolk

Mary Barker (née Royal), Liphook, Hampshire

Mr Everitt Barnes

Trevor J. Barnes, Blofield, Norfolk

Christopher Barrett, formerly Blofield

Ellen M. Basey-Fisher, Blofield, Norfolk

Mr Gerald and Mrs Janet Basey-Fisher, Blofield, Norfolk

James Batchelor, Blofield

Roy Batchelor, Weymouth

Frederick J.T. Bates, All Saints, Hemblington

Jeanette Bath, Brundall, Norwich

Kevin Baxter, Hemblington

Keith and Lynda Beck

Phyllis Becket, Bedford

The Beresford Family, Blofield, Norfolk

The Laurels Berrys

Betty, Lingwood, Norfolk

Gerald Bickers, Blofield, Norfolk

Geraldine Billington, Bedford/born in Blofield

Jeff and Amanda Bird, Blofield, Norfolk

Mrs A.D. Boast, Dussindale, Norwich

Helen R. Bradford, Acle, Norfolk

Mr and Mrs A. Bray, Blofield

The Broad Family, Pedham

Trish Brocklebank

Sue Brown and James Porter, Blofield Heath

Tracey Brown, Blofield

Arthur A. Browne, Blofield, Norwich

Vera Buckland, Brundall, Norfolk

Lucy Budgen

Mr E.J. Bulley, Blofield, Norfolk

Mrs H.M. Bulley, Blofield, Norfolk

Ray Bulley, Norwich

Joy B. Bunting, Blofield, Norfolk

Susan Jayne Burchan (née Knights), Blofield

Roderick and Susan Bushnell, Blofield, Norfolk

Freda Bussey, Blofield, Norfolk

Glenna J. Butler (née Rope), Blofield

Gail Buttifant, Drayton, Norfolk

Derek R. Buxton, North Walsham, Norfolk

Kim A. Buxton, Vardo, Norway

Jacqueline M. Byatt, Blofield Heath

Margaret Calver (White), Thorpe End

Emma Canfor, Blofield Heath

Peter and Margaret Canfor, Blofield Heath

Rachel Canfor, Blofield Heath

George C. Cann

Maurice and Marjorie Cann, Blofield

The Cardings, Blofield, Norfolk

Amelia Cardoe

Diana and Brian Carman, Hemblington, Norfolk

Susan S. Chandler (née Butler), Ash, Kent

Richard and Anne Churchill, Blofield Heath, Norfolk

Linda Clarke, Brundall

Alice Codling, Blofield, Norfolk

Emma Codling, Blofield, Norfolk

Louise and Richard Codling, Blofield, Norfolk

David and Glensy Cogman, Blofield Heath

John Conlin, Brundall/born in Blofield

Mrs Doris Cook (née Buckland), Norwich

Laurence and Sylvia Cooper, Blofield, Norfolk

Mary and Graham Cooper, Blofield

Nicholas Crane, Upton, Norfolk

Mrs Annick Crisford (née Rigby), Blofield, Norfolk

Joan P. Crisp, Blofield, Norfolk

Caroline and Niall Cullens, Petts Wood, Kent

Joe and Beryl Cullum, Buckenham, Norfolk

Cushion, Blofield, Norfolk

Pauline Cushion,

Mr P. Dale, Little Plumstead, Norfolk

Sarah Ann Dale, Brundall, Norfolk

Ruth Darby, Norwich, Norfolk

The Darby Family, Blofield, Norfolk

Graham R. Davey, Blofield, Norwich

Olive W. Davies, Hemblington, Norfolk

Mr Eric L. Dawson, Blofield

Frances Dawson, Pedham, Norfolk

R. and B. Dawson, Blofield, Norfolk

Sandra and Roy Daynes, Blofield, Norfolk

Colin C. Debbage, born in Blofield

Mrs Janet Debbage, Lingwood, Norwich

Roy Debbage, Blofield, Norfolk

Simon, Caroline, Catherine, James and Laura Dent, Blofield

Aart and Cora van Deutekom, Blofield

James Dewing, Brewster Court, Blofield

Mr K. and Mrs D. Durrant, Blofield, Norfolk

Sandra A. Durrant, St Andrews Way, Blofield

Chris and Anne Eastaugh (née Marriott), Blofield Village

Mrs J. Edmunds, Hemblington, Norfolk

Dr Rodney Edrich, Acle, Norfolk

Joan R. Edridge, Brundall, Norfolk

Jean Eldred, Cromer (Blofield 1977–1997)

K. Ellis, Blofield, Norfolk

Elaine and John Elvin, Blofield

Irene Faiers (née Houghton), Blofield, Norfolk

Peter A. Falgate, Old Catton, Norfolk

Brenda Falgate, Brundall, Norfolk

M. and S. Falvey, Blofield, Norfolk

Doreen Fleury, ex Blofield/now Cheam, Surrey

Mr Ron and Mrs Ann Fleury, Blofield, Norfolk

Dawn Folkard (née Batchelor), Blofield

Aubrey Forster, Blofield, Norfolk

Eric Forster, Blofield, Norfolk

Michael and Joan Fox, Blofield, Norfolk

Matthew Francis, Blofield Heath, Norwich

Mr Robert (Bob) J. Francis, formerly Blofield Heath/now Halvergate, Norfolk

Clifford Lewis Futter (deceased), Church Farm, Blofield, Norfolk
Helen M. Gallaway, Blofield, Norfolk
Ivor and Jane Garner, Blofield Heath, Norwich
Margaret R. Gedge, Blofield Heath, Norfolk
Sue and Chris Gedge, Blofield, Norfolk
Mary Elizabeth Gentle, Garden Road, Blofield
Nesta Getliffe, formerly Blofield
M.R. and J.R. Gilham, Blofield Heath, Norfolk
Betty and Eric Gladwin, Blofield, Norfolk
Eileen Goldsmith (née Bickers), Blofield
Mrs Margaret Goodrum, Hemblington
Mr F.S. Gowing, Blofield, Norfolk
The Gowing Family, Bradestone
Charmaine L. Graham, Cape Town, South Africa
Wilf Graver, Blofield, Norfolk
Mr W.J. Graver, Swaffham, Norfolk
Doreen L. Green, Blofield, Norfolk
Mrs Elizabeth A. Green, Brundall, Norwich
Violet Green, Blofield, Norfolk
Dorothy M. Griffin, Blofield, Norwich
Colin R. Hague, Blofield, Norfolk
Mr and Mrs D. Hale, Blofield, Norfolk
Margaret Hall (née Layt), Hellesdon, Norfolk
Rosemary Hammond, Blofield
B. Hanton, Blofield
The Harding Family, North Street, Blofield
B. and G. Hardy, Blofield, Norwich
Jonathan Hardy, Blofield, Norwich
Richard P. Hardy, Blofield, Norwich
Mr Derek Harper, Blofield
Philip, Benny, George, Laura and Henry Harston, West Lodge, Blofield
Michael and Sheila Harvey, Blofield Heath
Margaret and Eric Heard, Blofield
Hemblington C.P. School, Blofield Heath
Bruce and Molly Henderson-Gray, Blofield
Mr and Mrs T. Henwood, Blofield, Norfolk
John P. Herne, Poringland, Norfolk
Barbara A. Hilldrup, Blofield, Norwich
Mr Andrew R. Hilton, Dringhouses, York, Yorkshire
Helen Hipper, Blofield, Norfolk
Raymond Holland, Blofield, Norfolk

Adrian Hollis, formerly Blofield, Norfolk
Ian Hollis, formerly Blofield, Norfolk
Malcolm and Pamela Hollis
Melvin Hollis, formerly Shillito Road, Blofield
Douglas and Gloria Holmes, Blofield, Norfolk
Sally Horne, Cromer, Norfolk
Arthur (Ha'Penny) Horner, Norfolk
Douglas S. Horner, Blofield, Norfolk
Kenneth and Daisy Horner, Hemblington, Norfolk
Kenneth and Olwen Horner, Blofield Heath, Norfolk
Mr Peter Stanley Horner, Burndall, Norfolk
Stanley G. Horner, Blofield, Norfolk
Shirley and John Horton, Blofield Heath, Norwich
John L. Houghton, Norwich
John R. Howard, Church Alley, Blofield
Liz and Tony Howard, Blofield
Marie I. Howard, Church Alley, Blofield
Stephen Howard, H.C. Howard Builders, Blofield Heath
Charles S. Howes, Lingwood, Norfolk
Lambert, Elsie, Stanley Howes, Blofield, Norfolk
Carl and Wendy Hubbard, Moulton St Marys, Norfolk
Paul and Marion Hubbard, Norwich
Sheila (née Francis) and Terry Hubbard, Blofield, Norwich, Norfolk
Tom and Marion Hunnybun, Blofield Heath, Norfolk
Adelaide E.C. Hunter, Brundall, Norfolk
Andrew and Julie Hutchin, Horstead
Ann and John Hutchin, Blofield
Jamie and Michelle Hutchin, Blofield
Helen Hylton, Blofield
Myrtle Ingle (née Waterson), Blofield Heath
Brian and Margaret Ireland, Blofield
Oliver and Helen James, Blofield, Norfolk
Lynne H. Janes, North Walsham
Arthur Jermy, Hemblington, Norfolk
The Johnstone Family, Blofield, Norfolk
Jill Jones, Blofield, Norfolk
Frank and Jackie Kearns, Blofield Heath, Norfolk
Ivor Kemp, Hickling, Norfolk
John, Leonie and Trudy Kemp, Blofield

Barry and Jenny King, Norwich and Blofield Heath
Mr and Mrs D.R. King, Blofield, Norfolk
Jim King, born Blofield 23rd May 1917
Miss L. King, Hamptonwick, Surrey
Paul King-Ingham, Norfolk. Born in The Street, Blofield. 1926
Peter L. and Margaret A. Kirby, Blofield Heath
Susan Lamb, Blofield
Brian Lambirth, Blofield Heath
John and Irene Latham, Blofield
Len and Judy Layt, Little Plumstead, Norfolk
Jane L. Lennie, Blofield Heath, Norfolk
Mr Raymond J. Lindsay, Lingwood, Norfolk
S. Long, Blofield, Norfolk
B.W. and C.J. Lucking, Little Plumstead, Norfolk
Mr Andrew, Mrs Susanne and Miss Samantha Lynn, Blofield, Norfolk
Grant J. MacDonald, Blofield, Norfolk
Lisa M. MacDonald, Blofield, Norfolk
Andrew and Alexia Mack, Blofield, Norfolk
Katherine Lara Mack, Blofield, Norfolk
Michael Ian Mack
Michael and Zoe Mack, Blofield, Norfolk
Robert and Lois Mack, Blofield, Norfolk
Stephen John and Yvonne M.B. Mack, Blofield, Norfolk
Mr G. Mackerell, Blofield, Norfolk
Ben Mackintosh
Antonia Macpherson, Blofield, Norfolk
Helen, Philip and Katie Mahon, Blofield, Norfolk
Mrs Rita Marriott, Strumpshaw
Nicholas Matthews, Blofield, Norfolk
Chris and Sandy Mayes, Blofield, Norfolk
Doris L. Mayes, Blofield, Norfolk
David and Sara McCarthy, The Hollies, Blofield, Norfolk
Andrew McGregor, Shetland
Robert McGregor, Fife, Scotland
M.C. McManus, Blofield Heath
Christine McNamara, Strumpshaw, Norfolk
Maureen A. McNamara-Capes
Mrs Mara Miller, Phillip Ramsay and Caroline Ramsay, Blofield Heath, Norfolk

Frances Jayne Milliken, Blofield Heath, Norwich

Ann Mills, Blofield, Norfolk

P.B. and M. Mindham, Blofield Heath, Norfolk

Malcolm J. Minter, Thorpe St Andrew, Norfolk

Stephen, Sandra and Abbie Mitchell, S. & S. Mitchell Newsagents, The Street, Blofield

Grace Moore, Hemblington Hall

Julie Moore, Blofield Heath

James B. Morley, Blofield, Norfolk

Richard J. Morley, Newtongrange, Scotland

David K. Morton, North Burlingham, Norfolk

Mrs June Nelson (née Hilton), Fullerton, California, USA

Mike and Daphne Nicholls, Blofield Heath

Mrs Jill Nursey, Melton Mowbray, Leicestershire

John Oakley, Brundall, Norfolk

Bob and Hazel Offord, Blofield, Norfolk

Gay Olley, Blofield Heath, Norfolk

L. Olley, Blofield Heath, Norfolk

Dick Oosthoek, Blofield, Norfolk

Michael and Margaret Oxbury, Blofield, Norfolk

Nicholas and Sylvia Oxbury, Blofield, Norfolk

Simon, Donna, Christopher and Joshua Page, Blofield, Norfolk

Jean E. Palmer, Blofield, Norfolk

Lesley Parker, Brundall, Norfolk

The Parry Family, Blofield, Norfolk

Mrs Anne Parsley, Blofield, Norfolk

Wayne Patterson, Blofield, Norwich

Brenda Peart (née Layt), Brundall, Norfolk

Karen Petch (née Batchelor), Blofield

George and Joan Pickersgill

Tony Pitman, Blofield Corner, Norfolk

Mrs E.J. Place, Brundall, Norfolk

Audrey and Harold Plumbly, Blofield Heath, Norfolk

Neil Prior, Wreningham

Mrs Betty Pugh, Blofield, Norfolk

Mr and Mrs A.W. Purdy, Blofield, Norfolk

The Rant Family

Matthew Read and Alexandra Fegan Read, Blofield, Norfolk

Muriel Read, Blofield, Norfolk

Patricia M. Reynolds, Blofield, Norfolk

Dr John Rigby, Blofield, Norfolk

Daphne J. Rogers, Ixworth, Suffolk

Doreen A. Rogers

Janys E.M. Rogers, Swanton Morley, Norfolk

Adrian Rope, Blofield

Adrian and Jenny Rope, Blofield

Peter Rope, Dickleburgh, Norfolk

Richard Rope, Pulham Market, Norfolk

Roger R. Rope, Brundall, Norfolk

Stephen Rope, Blofield

Tony Rope, 3 Keys Garage, Blofield

Tony and Maria Rope, Street Farm, Blofield

Martel D. Rose

Malcolm R. Ross, Blofield Heath, Norfolk

Ian Rowarth, Watton, Norfolk

John and June Rowe, Blofield Corner

The Russells

Sarah J. Russen, Re: Hosier, Blofield, Norfolk

Beris Sampson, Pill, Bristol

Mr A. Sands, Pedham, Norfolk

Linda S. Sawyer (née Butler), Blofield

Dianne, Barrie, Meriel and Georgina Scott, Blofield Heath

Gerald Searle and Family, Blofield, Norfolk

Petra Searle, Blofield

Diana Sherring (née Hammond), Horley (Blofield 1944–66)

Marguerite E. Shreeve, Blofield Heath, Norfolk

Ray and Moira Shreeve, Blofield, Norfolk

Miss Rebecca Sibley, Blofield, Norfolk

Barrie Simpkins, Blofield, Norfolk

Neville Skedge, Thorpe St Andrews, Norwich

Mr Brian H. and Mrs Ann R.A. Smith, Blofield, Norfolk

E. and R. Smith, Blofield, Norfolk

Gwen Smith, Blofield Heath, Norwich

J. Susan Smith, Hemblington

Jane E. Smith, Blofield Heath

Kathleen F. Smith

Peter J. Smith, Blofield, Norfolk

Amy Snelling, Blofield

Michael Sowerby, Blofield, Norfolk

Gerhard Richard Spurgeon, St Andrews Way, Blofield

The Stanley Family, Blofield

Mr G.W. Stapleton, Brundall, Norfolk

Gary D. Starkings

Ian R. Starkings

Malcolm J. Starkings

Terry Starkings, Wood Farm, Hemblington

Anthony Taylor, Norwich, Norfolk

Michael Tedcastle, Blofield

Pat and Malcolm Thomas

Nancy Thompson (née Fuller), Blofield

Sylvia and Stuart Thompson, Blofield (33 years)

Dr Mark Todman and Janet Todman, Blofield, Norfolk

David Trett, Blofield, Norfolk

Mrs E.M. Trett, Blofield, Norfolk

Mr and Mrs Christopher Wace, Gables Court, Hemblington

Ray and Vera Wales, Blofield, Norfolk

Geoff and Eileen Walker, Blofield Heath, Norwich

John F.W. Walling, Newton Abbot, Devon

Gillian A. Ward, Langham Green, Blofield

Vera and John Wardle, Blofield 1948. Now Norwich

Jacqueline M. Ware, Blofield, Norwich

Peter C. Warner, Acle, Norfolk

Tracey Warren, Halstead, Essex

Andrew Waters, Colchester, Essex

Jim Waters, Halstead, Essex

The Waters Family, formerly of Callow Green, Blofield, Norfolk

Stanley and Vivienne Weavers, Brundall, Norfolk

Mike and Bridget Webb, Blofield Heath and Lingwood

Sid and Madge Webb, Blofield Heath

Hazel Westgate (née Moss), Hethersett, Norfolk

Mr Graham E. White, Globe House, Blofield

John Whittaker, Blofield

Malcolm Whittaker, Hassingham

Barbara Wildman, Blofield, Norfolk

Verdun and Joyce Willgress, Blofield, Norfolk

Dennis and Eva Williams, Blofield, Norfolk

Mrs Grace Williams, Blofield, Norfolk

Martin and Debbie Williams, Brundall

Nina and John Winter, North Street, Blofield

William John Williams, Blofield, Norfolk

David Keith Winter, North Street, Blofield

Aileen Withers

Cranston Withers

Eloise Withers-Kilburn

Dennis and Pat Wymer, Blofield, Norfolk

Ray and Jean Yaxley

Mrs Freda Zambra, Bournemouth, Dorset